ARTHUR D. RAYBIN

How to Hire the Right Fund Raising Consultant

Getting the most from your campaign

Taft Group
Washington, D.C.

Taft Group is the nation's leading technology-based information and service organization serving the needs of nonprofit organizations and institutions. The information division provides a wide array of data and publications in fund raising, marketing, management, career advancement, and communications. The Taft Group's professional services division provides needs assessment, telemarketing, financial development, and asset management services; executive search assistance; and advanced training to major institutions and nonprofit organizations worldwide.

How to Hire the Right Fund-Raising Consultant

Printed in the United States of America

90 89 88 87 86 85   6 5 4 3 2 1

Library of Congress Cataloging-in-Publication Data

Raybin, Arthur D.
  How to hire the right fund raising consultant.

  Includes index.
  1. Fund raising consultants—United States.
2. Fund raising—United States. I. Title.
HV41.5.R39 1986   361.7′068′1   85-30285
ISBN 0-914756-25-7

DEDICATION

This book is dedicated to the memory of my father, Dr. Nathan H. Raybin, who practiced and taught dentistry in Cleveland. His advice will never be forgotten:

- If you learn anything of value about your profession, write it down so that it can be shared with others.

- Make mistakes working for others, then work for yourself.

- If you can't do it well, don't bother.

- Never regret the money spent on buying shoes or paying tuition for your children; it's the real evidence of growth.

Some things, however, were beyond his comprehension. Fund-raising consulting was one.

TABLE OF CONTENTS

PART III. WORKING WITH THE CONSULTANT

LIST OF FIGURES

LIST OF TABLES

PREFACE

This is a how-to book. It is written for the volunteer leaders and staff members of gift-supported organizations who want to know how to choose—and then use—fund-raising counsel to assist in raising funds from private sources.

I was prompted to write this book after thinking back on my 13 years as a consultant. Our firm has worked with more than 115 institutions, mostly on capital campaigns with goals between $1 million and $100 million for construction and endowment. Some 115 other institutions have interviewed us and then chosen another firm for the assignment. At least half of the meetings with these 230 organizations have ended with the committee chairman asking, "Have we really asked the right questions? Do you think that we have half a chance?" Too often, in fact, the wrong questions were asked, the interviewing committee did not really know what the organization's needs were, and those charged with hiring counsel had no real concept of the role a consultant plays in fund raising.

The book is meant to be useful to experienced executives and trustees as well as those facing a fund-raising drive for the first time. Part I presents a general introduction to the role of the fund-raising consultant and to the general form of the client-consultant relationship. The process of interviewing and choosing the best-fitted consultant for your organization is the subject of Part II. Part III describes how a consultant will work with you and your staff to achieve your campaign goals during the stages of a campaign. The final part addresses the important question of the cost of using a fund-raising consultant, and closes with a chapter that is perhaps unique for a book of this kind—one written from the point of view of the consultant. The emphasis throughout the book is on conducting a capital campaign, but much of the information and advice, and many of the techniques and principles, are applicable to other types of drives as well.

As this book is being published, the fund-raising profession is marking two milestones—the recent 50th anniversary of the American Association of Fund-Raising Counsel, Inc., and the 25th anniversary of the National Society of Fund Raising Executives. The former organization is composed of consultants, the latter of institutional development officers. These two organizations represent the two sides of the client-consultant relationship. I hope that this book enhances, enriches, and strengthens that relationship.

This book came into print through a combination of forbearance of family members and the advent of word-processing technology. Using a portable COMPAQ® computer and MicroPro's WordStar® program, the task of assembling words and sentences into coherent chapters and sections was much easier than had been anticipated.

My deep appreciation is extended to those who read the manuscript and put up with the incessant pounding of the NEC and Epson® printers that accompanied us wherever travels took us for the better part of a year. Readers included W. Bradford, Peter B., and Deborah Wiley (my father-in-law, brother-in-law, and wife, respectively—all publishers or writers by family tradition, profession, and inclination); John H. Detmold and Maurice G. Gurin, senior statesmen in fund raising; and the staff members of our firm who criticized, applauded, and encouraged from beginning to end—Cecily Bastedo, Catherine H. Cumpston, Dorothy Dzamba, Louise G. Grayer, Sal Lorello, and Katharine H. Welling. Last but not least, a special thanks to my sons, John and Gregg, who have endured a lifetime of fund-raising talk and have had a continuing curiosity about what their father really did for a living.

David E. Sharpe, director of the books and references division of The Taft Group, and his associates deserve special credit for their commitment to the project and their wise approach to the chore of making a complex text more comprehensible for the reader. Finally, my deepest gratitude is extended to Peter Whitten, the skilled copy editor who forced me to connect concepts in logical sequence and explain every assertion so that the reader could cope with a complex subject.

Chappaqua, New York   A.D.R.
September 15, 1985

Part I
Raising Funds: You and Your Consultant

What is a fund-raising consultant? What can a consultant do for an organization that it cannot do for itself? Part I surveys the role of the fund-raising consultant in today's world of gift-supported institutions and sketches the general outlines of the working relationship between client and consultant.

Chapter 1

ENTER THE
CONSULTANT

In the beginning . . .

Every day, hundreds of organizations in the United States—large
ones and small, public and private—compete for the philanthropic
dollar. Total giving is reported to have amounted to $75 billion in
1984, and a panorama of the fund-raising scene reveals the gamut of
organizations involved in capital drives: The regional symphony in
New Haven, Connecticut, recruits staff and prepares for a campaign
for several million dollars of endowment, while the Metropolitan
Opera concludes a national drive with a goal of $100 million. The
University of Michigan, a public university that derives its basic
support from the state legislature, prepares for its next multimillion
dollar campaign, and Planned Parenthood of Westchester County,
New York, announces completion of its $1 million relocation drive.
No longer is it just the private schools, colleges, and hospitals that
seek funds. Increasingly, public institutions—state universities,
public schools, and libraries in particular—must raise substantial
funds to supplement shrinking government appropriations. For the
gift-supported institution, the capital campaign has become part of
the American way.

Most large capital campaigns rely on the guidance of a professional fund-raising consultant. Rescue Inc., a local ambulance
service in rural Vermont, recently authorized a consultant to study
the feasibility of a $2 million endowment drive. That study, based
on careful research and interviews, will predict if the goal is attain-

able, who the best donors are likely to be, and whether the organization's leadership is prepared for the task. Leaders of gift-supported institutions understand that the capital support for their organizations' missions is too important to be chanced to an intuitive or common-sense approach.

The fund-raising consultant brings special training and experience to the planning and management of a capital drive. Applying proven research methods and management theory, the consultant helps an institution achieve its capital goals—without actually soliciting contributions. Calling the consultant a "fund raiser" would, therefore, be a misnomer. The important distinction between a fund raiser and a fund-raising consultant is illustrated by Wolcott Street, whose career in professional fund raising spans a half-century. He likens the fund-raising consultant to a football coach:

> The real fund raisers are the volunteers—the chairmen and members of committees who actually ask for the money. The fund-raising counsel is not a solicitor. He is like the coach of a football team, who is paid for his ability to plan strategy and tactics and get the team members, who are *not* paid, to execute them. He does not get on the field and carry the ball. He sits on the sidelines and is successful in terms of his ability to motivate the players, to keep their enthusiasm at a high pitch, and to make things happen on the field according to the plan he has mapped out in which he has coached these volunteers.[1]

Drawing upon broad experience in other campaigns, the consultant can put your capital plans into perspective. As an outsider, the consultant can make impartial recommendations and focus on your financial needs without the distractions of day-to-day management of the organization.

WHAT IS A FUND-RAISING CONSULTANT?

Systematic fund raising dates back to the YMCA's first campaigns in the late 19th century. Colleges and hospitals followed the YMCA example after the turn of the century. By the 1920s, a handful of consulting firms had been established, marking the beginning of the fund-raising consulting profession. These new firms were often retained to help colleges and universities remain solvent during the difficult days of the Depression. In 1935 the American Association of Fund-Raising Counsel was founded, a sign that expertise in fund-raising was replacing the amateur's old-school-tie approach.

The fund-raising consultant has gained a permanent place in today's world of gift-supported institutions. There are at least 60 firms in the United States; 30 of them belong to the American Association of Fund-Raising Counsel (AAFRC), the industry's professional association. (Appendix A provides additional information on the AAFRC.) Additionally, many free-lance consultants provide services to smaller agencies and organizations.

Until recent years, most fund-raising consultants drifted into the profession from such diverse fields as advertising, public relations, teaching, and the ministry. Because the profession has grown in visibility and universities have begun to offer courses in fund raising, young consultants are now being trained more systematically. Still, the best preparation for a consulting career, and the kind of experience you should look for when hiring a consultant, is a stint or two as a development officer in a gift-supported organization. Experience on the other side of the desk puts a consultant in a better position to understand the needs of your organization.

Fund-raising consultants come in all sizes and shapes. Like most of the professions, fund raising has been dominated until recently by males. But women have begun to play a major role, and several have established firms. A glance through the AAFRC's membership directory reveals the diversity in the specialities, interests, and types of consultants available. This is a strength for the profession, but presents a possible pitfall for you. From among the great diversity of types and styles of consultants, you may be tempted to choose advisors with whom you are comfortable or who look and sound like you. Remember: The consultant you hire might on occasion have to be tough—to prod, goad, push, and sometimes say "no." If your relationship with counsel is too cozy, a productive, dynamic tension could be lost.

THE CAPITAL CAMPAIGN AND OTHER FUND-RAISING DEVICES

Organizations employ numerous approaches to raise money. Some conduct benefits, which might vary from a school auction that raises a few hundred dollars to a world-wide famine relief concert that might net $50 million. Little League raffles, church suppers, and buy-a-table political dinners are familiar ways to raise money locally. *Annual funds drives,* also known as budget or maintenance drives and in churches as every-member canvasses, encourage contributions on a yearly cycle to cover operating expenses for an organization. An ongoing program at many institutions is *planned giving,* which seeks to convince donors to include the organization in their wills or to consider other forms of less immediate giving. Contributions can provide an income to the donor for life from a principal sum, but upon the donor's death the principal reverts to the institution. All such plans are important sources of money for an organization. However, the major method of institutional fund-raising for long-term goals—and the focus of this book—is the *capital campaign.*

Most organizations conduct capital campaigns at the same time that they maintain annual giving programs, but the two programs are markedly different. Goals for a capital campaign, for example, are usually 10 to 20 times greater than the income from an annual campaign. And, unlike annual funds, which seek broad participation from as many donors as possible (causing some to call it "cookie jar money"), the capital campaign focuses on large contributions from a small number of donors. The emphasis in a capital campaign is on commitments so substantial that only a small percentage can make them. An organization with 5,000 members might focus on a mere 50 of them to obtain 80 to 90 percent of its projected goal, and within that small group, only five may account for half of all that is raised.

A simple story helps to illustrate the difference between annual giving and a capital campaign. A pig and a chicken were walking over a hill toward the next town, when the chicken saw a sign proclaiming: "The world's best ham and eggs—just ahead." Taking the pig in tow, the chicken said, "Let's go, I can hardly wait." The pig, holding back, replied, "Not me. For you it will be a contribution; for me it will become a total commitment."

THE SPECIAL ROLE OF THE OUTSIDER

The capital campaign being the unique project that it is, few organizations are willing to embark on one without the advice of a professional fund-raising consultant. Why? Sad experience has shown that an intuitive approach—setting goals that "felt right" and passing the hat to donors "who have always been with us"—has led to failure. In addition to experience from other drives, the consultant brings an equally important ingredient—objectivity.

Remaining objective is, indeed, one of the consultant's major contributions. When a board chairman claims that "raising $1 million will be a snap—we just need 1,000 people to give $1,000 each," someone must remind the chairman and committee that no such campaign exists in the annals of fund raising. Ordinarily, a "lead" commitment of $150,000 is required, followed by two at $100,000, four at $50,000, and so forth down to the $1,000 gifts. It is not easy to be the only voice crying out for reason when a board, college president, and staff are determined to go down a road to failure.

As you will see in later chapters, the consultant provides helpful guidance during the campaign by:

- maintaining a clear focus on the task and reminding all who are involved of the specific steps needed to complete it;

- insisting that the program be conducted in the appropriate sequence—if small gifts are made first, the larger commitments will never be achieved because the wrong standards will have been set;

- training the volunteers so they can effectively ask for the pledges;

- reminding both staff and volunteers that "apples and oranges cannot be mixed"—that this is a capital campaign and annual giving techniques do not apply.

Because the solicitation of funds is done by volunteers (not the consultants, remember), the consultant both trains the volunteers and provides ongoing guidance for them. Volunteers, with the best intentions, can get off the track; the outside consultant can remind them that:

- a complete organizational effort is still required so that the handful of primary prospects do not feel that they are being singled out from everyone else involved with the cause;

- it requires persistence to "make the case" to the top prospects and then to follow through with many additional visits until a "yes" is obtained and a letter of intent (or pledge card) signed;

- there are important techniques to apply (from what is said and how it is said during that first visit, to the written material submitted later, to dealing with other family members and determining how the donor's generosity will be recognized).

The consultant can give indispensable guidance at just the right time in a campaign. But remember: This help is possible because the consultant is an outsider, able to remain objective and to tell you what you need to know, not what might be comfortable to hear.

DECIDING ON A CAPITAL CAMPAIGN

In addition to the hundreds of organizations already engaged in capital drives, many more are looking at their financial needs and asking if a capital campaign is needed to meet them. Is this the best of times for a capital drive? The worst of times? Unfortunately, many development directors and boards of trustees will mistakenly conclude that the present (no matter when the present is) is the worst of times. They will give lots of reasons—the stock market is down, they will say, or the economy is not right, or impending tax reform will hurt giving, or competition for the philanthropic dollar is just too tight, or. . . .

One of the first services a consultant can give you is an assessment of the external environment for fund raising. In answer to the pessimistic views above, an experienced consultant would explain:

- *The stock market.* Ups and downs in the Dow Jones have little lasting impact on contributions. Surprisingly, large pledges are made when the market is rising but are not paid in full until a market decline begins. That way, as a donor's holdings continue to increase in value, the commitment costs even less from current income and capital; when the market will probably go no higher, the donor takes his profit and redeems the pledge.

- *Economic conditions.* Organizations will suffer if they delay major fund-raising programs every time there is a blip in the leading economic indicators. During the past 80 years, year-to-year declines in philanthropic giving have occurred only twice, once during the Depression and the other again just after World War II. In a recession the smaller agencies, schools, and churches hold back. Harvard, Yale, and Princeton forge right ahead and divide a pie that has fewer eaters!

- *Tax reform*. If it appears that changes in the tax code will have a negative impact on philanthropy, prudence would dictate moving forward with a fund-raising program before the new rules are enacted. However, no tax changes have had a lasting, negative impact on charitable contributions. Many Americans will generously support institutions in which they believe regardless of whether they realize significant tax deductions. During the past two decades, every change in the rules has had a demonstrably stimulating impact on philanthropy as new instruments for giving have been developed.

- *Competition*. "There are just too many campaigns being conducted in town right now; we should wait our turn." That cry fails to recognize the deep-seated American habit that leads individuals, families, foundations, and corporations to support the institutions they care about the most—no matter what others are doing elsewhere. In fact, when the philanthropic climate is highly charged in a community by a number of simultaneous campaigns, two things happen: More donors begin to think in larger terms about their favorite institutions due to the examples being set by neighbors; and the total amount being contributed to all causes rises.

Is now the time for your organization to undertake a capital campaign? This book will help you to answer that question. And if you answer in the affirmative, the following chapters will help you to understand what a fund-raising consultant can (and cannot) do for you, how to find the consultant who best fits your campaign, and how to work with that consultant for maximum success.

NOTE

1. Wolcott D. Street, *A Beacon for Philanthropy. The American Association of Fund-Raising Counsel through Fifty Years: 1935-1985* (New York: The American Association of Fund-Raising Counsel, 1985), 11.

Chapter 2

THE ROLE A CONSULTANT PLAYS: AN OVERVIEW

Can consultants really do any more than borrow my watch and then tell me what time it is?
—An old saw about outside "experts"

In some campaigns a timekeeping service would be well worth the cost! If consultants did no more, their contribution would be significant. Meeting deadlines is a problem for any fund-raising program, and few organizations are able to maintain a timetable on their own. Gradually, as things slide and as solicitors wait for the "right moment" to make a fund-raising call or hold a meeting, slippage occurs. If a campaign can be cut from 24 months to 18 with guidance from an experienced consultant, savings in staff expense and volunteer time—not to mention how much more the dollars paid on early pledges will be worth over those paid at the end of a protracted drive—can be significant. So one should not gainsay the value of a consultant who enforces a schedule on your campaign.

But, frankly, as important as timekeeping is, a consultant offers more important services to your organization. This chapter surveys the broad shape of the consultant-client relationship and describes briefly two of the consultant's most important functions—conducting the precampaign study and developing the campaign's case statement. The precampaign study phase is described in detail in chapter 9.

9

TYPES OF CONSULTING RELATIONSHIPS

In general, there are two basic types of consulting relationships:

- A firm can be engaged to conduct a precampaign study and then, if the response indicates that a drive is possible, provide *resident direction* for the campaign's duration—or at least until the goal is in sight. This means that the consultant, or a member of the consultant's staff, will be on the scene to provide staffing. If you engage a firm, one of its senior members will supervise the staff member assigned to you and will be present for important meetings.

- As more institutions develop staff strength of their own, firms are often asked to provide *counseling only*. In these instances, a precampaign study is conducted in the usual manner, then senior officers of the consulting firm provide guidance and direction for the program during weekly visits and meetings.

The second approach has benefits for both sides. Even a small institution should have an in-house development capability, and staff should be trained during a campaign to carry on the development effort later at more sophisticated levels of activity. From the firm's point of view, it is increasingly difficult to recruit and retain resident directors who are willing to move frequently from assignment to assignment—without really having a home base.

Some institutions prefer long-term relationships with outside counsel, working with the same firm for a decade or more. During a period of intensive campaign activity, the consultant devotes more time and attention to the organization. Many firms have shied away, for several good reasons, from associations of this type. There is a tendency for counsel to become too friendly and comfortable to address the client's real needs. Time pressures, so necessary in fund raising, tend to evaporate in a long-term relationship. And, it becomes increasingly difficult to suggest fresh approaches, new techniques, or even a complete change in course. It might be useful to retain a consultant for two or three years—enough time to get your institution through a capital campaign, build a significant annual support effort, and establish a planned-giving program— and then part company. Of course, the reward for a consultant comes when an invitation is offered for a return engagement several years later to assist with yet another capital campaign.

Whatever relationship you have with a consultant—short-term or long, resident or counseling only—it must be built on trust. If your organization does not trust counsel, the wrong people have been retained. I recall a wise campaign chairman once telling a querulous headmaster, "For gosh sake, Joe, we're paying the firm to help us raise a significant amount of money in any way that they can—and not to account for every moment of their time." The headmaster, excessively worried about getting full return on his investment in counselor, had been demanding time-consuming accounting of the consultant's time.

If an organization over-analyzes its relationship with counsel, fund raising invariably suffers. Consultants should not be your primary focus. One consultant, asked when he tired of his relationship with a new client, replied: "Just as soon as the ink on our contract no longer smudges." No doubt his response was the result of a difficult experience with an organization wanting terms spelled out in such a precise way that it became impossible to retain flexibility and spontaneity. Wise organizational leaders know that consultants are most effective when they do not feel constrained to meet arbitrary standards and deadlines. They must be in a position to change the ground rules and adopt new tactics when conditions change (revised needs, for instance, or slow response from major prospects, or delays in obtaining zoning clearances for a new building). Such changes can occur only when client and consultant share respect and trust.

THE PRECAMPAIGN STUDY: THE KEY TO FUND RAISING

When approaching a capital campaign, you and your organization must ask several questions:

☐ 1. Is our case compelling and urgent?

☐ 2. Can our goal be reached?

☐ 3. Is leadership available to guide the program and call on prospects?

☐ 4. Can the task be completed within a reasonable period?

☐ 5. Are individual components of our goal appealing, and to which prospects and at what levels of support?

The answers to these questions come from the precampaign study conducted by your consultant.

Techniques were developed nearly 50 years ago to "test the waters" for an institution through a feasibility study. This process, preceding a campaign, consists of confidential interviews (by the consultant) with a sample of the organization's constituency to determine how potential donors might respond to an appeal. Today, this approach has become a standard operating procedure for fund-raising consultants. Although the term "marketing" is not widely used, the study process is similar to what advertising agencies have developed for their clients to test consumer receptivity to a new product.

During confidential, in-person interviews with at least 25-100 of those people most supportive of an organization, the consultant learns whether or not "good will" is likely to lead to hard dollars in a fund-raising campaign. If the response is negative, a qualified consultant will be able to explain what must be corrected and how long it should take before a campaign becomes feasible. Problems might entail lack of available leadership (a weak board, perhaps), internal management difficulties, the absence of a convincing case, lack of visibility and understanding of the organization, competing drives in a community for similar causes, or low philanthropic priority on the part of board members.

Over the years, refinements have been made in feasibility study formats, and now the interviews usually lead to: 1) determination of what goal can be reached (plus or minus 10 percent); 2) which specific components of your general goal appeal to which prospects; 3) who will give and at what levels; 4) which solicitor should call on which prospect—and ask for how much toward which need; 5) how the campaign's message should be conveyed; and 6) how the program should be structured and who should lead it.

As you see, the information gathered from the precampaign study is the foundation of the campaign to come.

When you retain counsel for a study, the contractual agreement is usually separate from any arrangements to provide ongoing assistance for a later campaign. You would not ordinarily make a long-term commitment at this time. You would just agree, at first, to a short period of assessment—usually no more than 90 days. Some organizations feel that they might want to engage one firm for the study and another for campaign counseling, but this leads to many problems. Only the firm conducting the study is really in a position to render well-grounded advice. The interviewer learns a great deal about the organization's prospective donors and can advise you later about which solicitor will be the most effective in any situation, how much to ask for, and which component of the objectives list will be most compelling.

You may be tempted to authorize a study when you have no intention of proceeding with a campaign, no matter how positive the study results are. Several of your board members may just want to "test the water." Because study results become dated within several months of the interviews (prospects move to other interests, suffer economic reversals, divorce, remarry, or even die), time and money are wasted if an institution does not intend to have a campaign follow a positive study report. After all, the organization's needs and aspirations have been "telegraphed" to constituents, and momentum is already building as a result of the interviewing process.

IS A STUDY ALWAYS NEEDED?

A study might not be needed at all if the consultant has worked with the organization on a recent drive. But the possibility of a new campaign does raise a host of questions to ask yourself:

1. Are our objectives still really attractive?

2. Are the major donors ready to pledge again?

3. Is adequate leadership available?

It almost always makes sense to survey the field once more if constituents have not been interviewed in four or five years by an outsider. However, it may be unnecessary to have another study conducted if the consultants' role will be limited to providing assistance on a relatively small matter such as upgrading annual giving or developing a planned gifts program. Here are types of situations in which study interviews can turn up important information on ways to proceed:

13

- *Annual support (to meet the yearly operating budget).* For the past decade a school has had a "giving club" offering special recognition for contributions of $1,000 or more. As the realization sinks in that these contributions are worth only half that much today, debate ensues about increasing the minimum level to $1,500 or $2,000. More often than not, a brief study encompassing 10-15 interviews by a consultant will reveal that most of these donors have been waiting for the school to propose just such an upward adjustment. So there is no need to guess about constituent reactions and responses. Furthermore, the institution can tell all of its friends that the change is being made after a representative sample was asked for comments. The decision has not been made on an arbitrary basis.

- *Planned giving.* The board of a church has been considering a program for the past few years to encourage members of the congregation to include bequests in their wills for an endowment fund. Plans have not been implemented because no one knows how the message should be conveyed to members—or how they will react when they receive it. Here, too, a brief study will lead to information on which sound judgments can be made. (Should the minister or key lay leaders approach the best prospects? What type of material on the program should be printed?) It is likely that members have wondered why the board has not taken an active role in building the church's endowment through bequests! And the interviews will probably indicate that several individuals have already made planned gift arrangements that can be used to give others examples to follow.

Organizations that have not been through the study process in preparing for a capital campaign often ask if their staff members or board members could conduct the interviews themselves. They cannot and *should* not. Experience has shown that interviewees feel more comfortable with outsiders who can guarantee that responses will not be attributed and that confidentiality will be maintained. Furthermore, insiders lack experience in interviewing procedures and are hardly in a position to listen with objectivity to what is being said. Recognizing that they will have to live with the insiders for years to come, and will soon be involved with them in a campaign, the interviewees will not be candid in their responses.

THE CRUCIAL CASE STATEMENT

As you will see in chapter 3, when you look into the possibility of beginning a capital campaign there are several tasks to be accomplished long before you think about retaining a consultant. One of those tasks is to develop a long-range plan about where your organization is going and why you need capital funds to get there. This plan will gradually evolve into a compelling *case statement*. Your campaign cannot be taken to prospective donors until an effective case statement has been drafted. This document sets forth your long-range plan in a fund-raising context. In no more than 12-15 pages, this vital piece must explain several things about your institution:

• Why it was founded and what its mission has been
• Where it stands today
• Plans for the future
• The difference, in both quantitative and qualitative terms, additional funds will make
• How the organization intends to obtain the required funds

Although the first draft of the case statement emanates from your earliest planning, one of your consultant's key services will be to help you refine the case statement and put it into its ultimate form.

Assembling the case statement is as much process as it is substance. It evolves over several stages of your campaign until it is eventually published for the public (see figure 2-1). If the campaign leadership is not involved in reviewing this document at all stages of development, it will be difficult for those key people to convince others that the case supports the need for substantial contributions. The consultant's first exposure to the case is during the hiring interview, when your selection committee presents it for the first time to an outsider. If your organization has completed a thorough planning process, it should be able to explain its case to the prospective consultant. If it is not "larger" than the institution (meaning: Is it important not just to this organization, but beyond its walls or campus to a much more extended community?), trouble may lie ahead. If a board wants to build dormitories for a college that has had declining enrollment, the case is not very compelling. Wishful thinking does not make a case. From that initial interview with the selection committee, consultants will be asking themselves:

1. Does this case hold water?

2. Is it airtight?

3. Do we agree that it is both valid and compelling?

4. Is it really going to be "larger than the institution"?

5. Is the timing right (to win substantial support for it)?

6. Will anyone care?

7. Will leadership for a campaign be available and enthusiastic?

8. Has the planning process, leading up to a formulation of preliminary objectives, been as thorough as it should be?

Of course the consultant cannot attempt to answer these questions until the comprehensive feasibility study has been undertaken.

FIG. 2-1: The making of a case statement

Long-Range Plan

Preliminary Draft of Case Statement

Refining of Material Based on Counsel's Pre-Campaign Study

Successive Re-Drafts by Staff With Board and Leadership Review

Final Draft Used as "Campaign Prospectus" For First Solicitations

Case Evolves Into a Brochure for Campaign's Public Phase

Chapter 1 stressed the value of the consultant bringing an objective view to your campaign. As an outsider, the consultant challenges some of your most cherished views about your own institution. A college president's perspective on an institution, for example, might not fit with the view held by alumni. Counsel can provide much wisdom at this point, and it falls to the outsider to assemble the next draft of the case statement—without hyerbole, inappropriate adjectives, and first-person pronouns. Ultimately, it may take a dozen drafts to develop an acceptable piece that convincingly represents an institution.

Ultimately, the case will become a printed brochure. The original typed draft is for inner "family" prospects seen in the nucleus-fund effort only. The best approach is for the consultant to work with your development officer, public relations people, and designer. Much is lost if the development officer attempts to interpret the precampaign study results to the designer; counsel should do it directly in a meeting with all who will be responsible for the brochure. The published version of the case statement serves several purposes:

- Training material for all solicitors—so that they will feel competent to tell the story and ask for the gift

- Back-up, "leave-behind" material for the project—after the fund-raising visit has been completed

- Source document from which other campaign pieces are developed—audio-visual productions, proposals for foundations and corporations, and presentations for individual donors

The precampaign study and the case statement—these are two important ingredients in a successful drive. Whether you use a consultant for resident direction or for counseling only, they are among the most valuable services provided by counsel.

Part II
Hiring a Consultant

Finding the right fund-raising consultant for your organization is a step-by-step process, beginning with the development of long-range plans and capital needs. Part II describes the steps you must take to narrow the list of potential consultants, interview prospects, evaluate candidates, reach a final choice, and sign a contract. The emphasis throughout Part II is on matching your needs with the right consultant.

Chapter 3
GETTING STARTED

On your mark, get set, go!

This short chapter is a checklist of the several things you must do before beginning to search for a consultant. Prior to retaining professional counsel, you must lay important groundwork. Although the consultant you hire can tell you how to reach your goals, only your organization can determine what those goals should be. And your organization's board and important leaders must be unanimously behind those objectives. If you do not accomplish the important preparatory steps, your ultimate task—finding and using a fund-raising consultant—will be difficult. And you will waste a lot of time later on trying to find the right consultant—or, worse, choosing the wrong one.

There is no formula for moving an organization toward considering a capital campaign. More often than not, it is the chief executive officer (president, headmaster, executive director) who senses that the gift-supported institution needs a long-term plan that will require infusions of capital. With the support of at least one key board member, and usually with the aid of the development officer, the institution's head must lead the organization through several steps of a preliminary survey before thought can be given to the fund-raising side and the retaining of counsel:

□ 1. Formulate the long-range plan with the participation of development staff, professional staff (faculty, medical staff, etc.), and board members.

□ 2. Discuss the long-range plan with the full board, then revise it—over and over, if necessary—until everyone is satisfied. (This plan will evolve into the eventual case statement for the campaign.)

□ 3. Affix costs to each element of the plan.

□ 4. Determine what parts of the plan must come first if all of the needed funds are not available. (This is usually a task for the board.)

□ 5. Review records of prior campaigns to gain a sense of what the institution has achieved in fund raising.

□ 6. Achieve agreement that the priority items are urgent and that only a capital campaign can provide the needed funds.

□ 7. Appoint a selection committee.

When you have completed these steps you will have done considerable work. However, the picture of your campaign will still be blurry—your financial estimate will not be exact, your case statement will still be in a formative stage, and costs for executing the campaign will not be established. But attention can now be turned to the question of whether the financial resources exist within the constituency to achieve the desired goal. And because you have prepared to this point, the consultant's expertise can help to clarify the picture. The search for counsel can begin.

Chapter 4

FROM PROSPECT LIST TO INTERVIEW

> *Why don't we ask all of the firms listed in the* Yellow
> Pages *under "Fund-Raising Consultants" to submit
> proposals? We can interview the ones who make the
> best pitch.*
> —A board member who knows better how to
> buy products than services

It would be impractical, and quite expensive, to interview all 60 fund-raising firms in the United States, or even the 30 firms belonging to the AAFRC. And those numbers don't include the many hundreds of individual consultants. The selection committee's first task, then, is to create a short list of firms that are likely candidates.

THE CONSULTANT SELECTION COMMITTEE

The selection committee should be small; five, perhaps, is the right number. At least two members should have prior experience in major campaigns and in working with outside consultants. It is useful to include one skeptic who doubts the campaign's chances for success or the wisdom of using a consultant. The committee should be representative of the board at large. That way, prospects understand the governance group, and the full board will be satisfied that the selection process has taken all points of view into account. Your organization's chief executive officer and development officer should be *ex officio* members of the group. If your organization is small, or your board members lack experience with consultants, it would make sense to include one or two individuals who have been through a capital campaign but are not trustees.

CREATING A PROSPECT LIST

Determine Possibilities

To obtain information and initial references about prospective consultants, the committee can turn to several sources:

- Institutions similar to your own that have been through fund-raising programs can share their experience and suggest firms.

- Associations to which your organization belongs will have suggestions.

- The American Association of Fund-Raising Counsel, Inc., in New York, provides information on firms that offer the type of services being sought. The AAFRC publishes an annual membership directory.

- Volunteer leaders of other organizations in your community may recommend consultants.

- Development officers at institutions with which your leaders are associated (a college, for instance), might suggest a specific firm.

- Your state's central offices for registering charities and consultants, or for consumer protection or trade, may have listings of fund-raising firms or individuals, complete with filings, where required, of fund-raising results and contracts.

- Your local library is a source of useful directories and magazines, such as *Fund Raising Management* magazine.

Review Possibilities

In narrowing your list of possibilities, you should evaluate several factors in the order that follows.

Size and style. Once you have compiled your long list of possibilities, take a look at it. Your first two considerations should revolve around size and style—do you want a large firm with plenty of back-up support, a smaller organization, or even a sole practitioner? And what do you prefer in a firm's style—should it be formal or easy-going, intense or casual?

Experience. Consider how experience relates to the initial campaign survey for your organization. Should you insist on a firm that has had experience with organizations like yours? Small firms tend to develop their own specialties; the larger ones have several kinds of specialists. While experience in a given field is often useful, there are times when an institution needs a fresh approach. If a series of past campaigns for a hospital have all looked alike, it might be wise for the hospital's board to consider a consultant with, say, extensive college experience but who is not hampered with preconceptions about how medical drives are conducted.

Empathy with your cause. Should you be concerned that the prospects be sympathetic to your institution's mission? Believe it or not, it really does not matter. In fact, the less emotionally involved counsel is, the easier it is to be objective and dispassionate about your fund-raising problems. Of course, the extreme opposite would also be silly—a Planned Parenthood affiliate could not be represented by a consultant who personally opposes all means of contraception.

Credentials. As the final step in narrowing your list of prospects, you will want to carefully check any initial references you have gathered. At this stage it is necessary only to be certain that firms on your now short prospect list are reputable. A consulting firm's best credential is membership in the American Association of Fund-Raising Counsel, Inc., for the AAFRC membership committee reviews the firm's involvement with every client over a five-year period before the firm is granted admission. In many of the larger states, fund-raising firms and individual consultants are required to register with a central office (such as the Office of Charities Registration of the Department of State in New York or the Department of Consumer Protection in Connecticut). Many states require that firms be bonded as well as registered. In most instances, "registration" calls for an annual filing of results in all fund-raising programs undertaken for clients as well as filing of contracts before new assignments are started.

FROM LIST TO INTERVIEWS

When you have reduced your list of prospective consultants to a half-dozen or so, you have your short list. Resist the temptation to interview those six. The committee will have no sense, at the end of the process, of what was discussed or how the firms compare. A bit more homework and reference checking can get your list to three, a manageable number of interviews.

Exchange Information

Ask the competing firms to send material on their general approach to fund raising, staff capability, and clients past and present. In turn, it is helpful to send them a copy of your long-range plan.

Brief the Prospect

It may be helpful for a member of the committee to privately brief a representative of each firm. This session may eliminate firms from the list. Some will decide that they cannot provide the assistance you need; others will be screened out by your interviewer, who will quickly recognize a bad fit. Not only can you initially screen your prospects, but the consultant can initially screen you. For more on the questions a consultant might ask you, see chapter 15.

Schedule the Interview

Each of the final contending prospects should be interviewed on separate days in sessions that last about 90 minutes. This allows you sufficient opportunity to understand the approach and style of each one. Similarly, an unrushed atmosphere enables the consultants to learn about your institution and be able to make a careful presentation. More often than not, one interview with the committee will be adequate for making the choice. If you expect that it will take two rounds, let the prospects know at the outset.

Tell each prospect how long the interview will last, who will be present, and what ground is to be covered. Be sure that each firm is represented by the persons who will actually be doing the work. If they are not available, make it clear to the firm that you will have to meet those individuals at some time during the selection process. It makes little sense to learn of a firm's general approach; you need to know who will be assigned later on to implement a study and the campaign plans.

Some organizations will ask a consultant to submit a proposal in advance of the meeting. Even if there has been an earlier briefing, however, a prospect cannot know enough about an organization and its requirements to prepare a useful proposal prior to the interview. Further, it makes no sense to request long proposals from consultants who will soon be eliminated from consideration. A full proposal should follow the interview, not precede it.

Never at dinner: a consultant's experience. I remember one situation in which a clever executive director felt that the interview process could be shortened by having three firms make their presentations as follows: the first at cocktails, the second at dinner, and the third over coffee. She thought she would save time for busy trustees; in reality, everything was a mess. My presentation was first, over cocktails. When I finished my discussion, a trustee said, "Let's go to dinner, and we'll ask you a few more questions." The staff officer had to interject, "No, he's the 'cocktail' firm, and we have someone else to see at dinner." Everyone was a bit embarrassed. Later, I learned that the committee could not reach a decision and that a consultant would not be selected for at least six months.

Chapter 5

THE INTERVIEW

*Are you ready for today's "beauty parade"—
appearances by consulting firms every half hour? Do
you think that this group will know how to make a
decision?*
—Comment made by a consultant as he completed his meeting with a selection committee

An effective selection committee will avoid a "beauty parade," but
will conduct its interviews with carefully prepared questions that
force a firm to reveal its strengths and weaknesses

WHAT IS REALLY IMPORTANT?

Using carefully prepared questions, you can gather lots of information about a prospect during an interview. From that information
you will be trying to answer these questions:

- Will this consultant understand us and mesh well with our
  constituents?

- On the other hand, will the consultant be too comfortable
  (fine for the study but unable to push and prod us later)?

- How flexible are these people? How will they react when
  everything—needs, goals, public relations problems—
  changes during the study or the campaign itself?

- Will we have confidence in the prospect's recommendations
  and be willing to act on advice given?

- Do we *really* know what this will cost?

- Will the consultant give in too easily when we push back?

- Is the prospect too classy (or too dull) for our constituents? Either way, will it make any difference in how much we raise or how long it takes to raise it?

Mutual respect: a consultant's experience. The chairman of one selection committee let me know in advance that we were being interviewed because we had a reputation for being tough, for pushing what we believed to be the most successful approach no matter how many board members initially objected. So we acted accordingly during the interview and won the assignment. Later, another board member said that the chairman had told him, following the interview: "We need him to do the job for us, but I certainly wouldn't want him as a luncheon companion." The lesson is clear. Consultants must prefer respect over camaraderie. And you too must be prepared to choose the consultant you respect, not just the one you find personable and friendly.

STARTING THE INTERVIEW

The Setting

Conducting an interview as graciously and comfortably as possible is important. If you sit at one end of a long table and the consultants sit at the other, a we-they situation is created. Intentionally or not, the interviewee will be on guard. A better plan is to leave vacant chairs interspersed with those of the committee. The consultants will feel part of the group—a sentiment necessary if the two parties are to work together.

Opening Statement and Review

Begin the interview by explaining what your institution is all about and where you hope it is headed, including the preliminary planning that preceded this meeting. Then the consultants should be asked to provide background on their firm and the general approach they would take in working with the organization. But do not dawdle here—both sides can accomplish this in about 15 minutes. You want to move quickly to your key questions.

SAMPLE INTERVIEW QUESTIONS—STRONG AND WEAK RESPONSES

Your questions should be prepared in advance—not just to provide the committee with a check-list, but because you want to be sure to cover the same ground with each firm. When developing your questions, you will, of course, want to find out what the prospect will do and how work with the prospect will proceed. However, keep in mind that you can learn as much by seeking out what consultants *will not* do—will they be pushed and intimidated by your board or stand up for what's prudent and wise? Will they recognize new input and adjust, or proceed blindly with the initial plan? Following is a set of sample interview questions, along with examples of "strong" or "weak" responses you might hear. Of course, these questions are only models, not the exact set you will prepare. Comments on the responses appear when appropriate.

QUESTION: Tell us what you have done in situations similar to ours.

Strong
Response:
Institution X, with a similar donor base, had never raised more than $2 million, but its long-range plan called for $7 million. In the study interviews we pointed this out, worked at raising sights, and watched key donors talk themselves into viewing the institution from a fresh perspective.

Weak
Response:
Every situation is very different. You are talking about a school; we have done a museum that seems similar in size, scope, and need.

Comment:
The strong response deals with fund-raising tactics and the institution's concerns; the weak response speaks to types of institutions and has nothing to do with what is really bothering the committee.

31

QUESTION: What would you do if your interviews did not seem to be providing conclusive evidence about giving potential?

Strong
Response:
We would meet with you quickly to see if the interview questions were creating a problem, if the preliminary goals could be stated differently, or if we were seeing the wrong people.

Weak
Response:
Once you get started, all of the interviews must be completed so that we can give you an accurate report.

Weak
Comment:
The weak response shows lack of flexibility and more interest in producing a product (report) than in helping an organization raise money.

QUESTION: If we were to engage your firm, who would be working with us?

Strong
Response:
Those of us here for the meeting today.

A study director on our staff—with whom you would meet before we began our work, of course.

Weak
Response:
It's difficult to tell right now; it really depends on who is available when we are asked to serve.

Comment:
In a matter of such importance to the institution, wouldn't you want to know who would be making the first approach to the important prospects?

QUESTION: Have you had any failures?

Strong
Response:
Yes. We are on target with our projections about 85 percent of the time; at institution Y we were convinced from interview responses that the case was well-received and compelling. In the drive itself we found that donors felt no sense of urgency about the matter. We had misread their comments.

At institution Z, only half of its goal was realized during the campaign; the second 50 percent dribbled in over the following two years. We had misread the constituency's readiness for the drive.

Weak
Response: Campaigns do fall short every now and then, but the reasons are almost always unpredictable—the lead donor dies, there is a change in staff leadership, or the volunteers don't cooperate.

Comment: If the consultants can't figure out why things went wrong elsewhere, how will they ever recognize mistakes and profit from them?

QUESTION: What would you do if a donor made negative comments in the study about this organization's leadership?

Strong
Response: We would encourage interviewees to meet with the board's head, unless it was that person who was the problem—then we would meet, on a confidential basis, with that person.

On more general matters, we would go back to the committee that had selected our firm.

Weak
Response: Nothing, until we covered the problem in our written report to the trustees.

QUESTION: Do you provide resident direction? Will we need it?

Strong
Response: Yes, we do, if it is needed.

No, we don't; if you are clear in your minds that you will need it, we are not the firm to select.

Weak
Response: Yes, and every institution really needs it.

No. There's good reason to feel that it is not required by any institution.

QUESTION: Will you prepare all of the printed material for our program?

Strong
Response:

Yes, we are a full-service firm.

No, we just counsel. Of course, we help in drafting material and work closely with your staff and outside publications people; but we want to focus first and foremost on fund raising, which is our specialty.

Weak
Response:

Of course; we can do just about anything you ask of us.

No, we don't like to get involved with printed material.

Comment:

How would you feel if the internist who diagnosed the need for surgery offered to perform the operation himself, instead of referring the case to a surgeon?

QUESTION: How long will it take? Will you be able to speed things up for us?

Strong
Response:

Studies usually take three months; this much time is needed if they are to be done properly. The campaign to follow might take as long as nine months to complete.

If we try to go faster, we may well miss some of the best prospects—or not give them enough time to reach thoughtful and generous decisions.

Weak
Response:

We can go through each step just as rapidly as you request.

If there is a reason to rush, we'll just cut back on the number of interviews.

Comment:

The strong answers acknowledge valid and important considerations; the weak responses demonstrates lack of integrity, judgment, and professionalism.

QUESTION: Do our basic objectives make sense to you? How would you express them differently?

Strong
Response:
Please give us a few days to rework the list and set it forth in terms which might make more sense to those being interviewed.

The categories are confusing.

Let's separate endowment and construction items.

Weak
Response:
They are just fine and we know that interviewees will react well.

QUESTION: What about competing campaigns of other institutions with the same constituents?

Strong
Response:
If you really don't need the funds now, consider delaying the study.

If the need is urgent, we will find out in the study if the competition is overwhelming or if all ships in the community will be lifted on the same rising tide.

Weak
Response:
Don't worry about them.

QUESTION: Can you tell us what really happens during a study interview?

Strong
Response:
Yes. Let me give you the basic questions we would ask, so the committee can go through a simulation of the process right now.

Weak
Response:
You are so unique that we would need a week to figure out what to ask.

Comment:
An inability to think quickly and act accordingly will hurt the cause when and if the weak response consultant is out in the field conducting interviews.

QUESTION: Why can't we start without a study?

Strong
Response:

Faced with a similar situation in business, would you proceed without a market analysis?

Do you really want to make an investment of time and money without an objective evaluation of the odds?

Weak
Response:

If you insist, we will be glad to plunge right into a campaign with your organization, provided it is clear that we are not responsible for the feasibility of the goal.

Comment:

Who would want a consultant who didn't stand up for the right way?

QUESTION: How much will all this cost? How would you expect to be paid, and when is each installment due?

Strong
Response:

Our fee would be x dollars for the study, approximately y dollars in expenses, and z dollars for counseling. We will spell out, in writing, what you can expect from us in each stage.

For the study, we would want one-third of the fee at the outset, and then payment of the balance as follows.

Weak
Response:

Well, our study fee will be x, but it is not possible to estimate how high expenses will go. Then there are a few extra charges for a campaign plan and for a case statement.

Of course we would expect most of the estimated total before we began.

Comment:

Straight talk and honest answers, such as the strong response, are needed when the subject is money. If you don't understand what is being said or meant, move on to the next candidate.

QUESTION: Is this an appropriate assignment for your firm? Do you have time to do it?

Strong
Response:
Yes, we have the time, and staff is available. We have done similar projects and will be able to bring much useful experience to bear.

Our experience with similar situations is limited, but our record indicates that we do well in new areas, and we would bring our best efforts to this assignment.

Weak
Response:
We can squeeze it in—no problem.

Our firm does well, no matter what the field.

QUESTION: Is there potential for a conflict of interest if you work with us and continue, at the same time, to provide assistance for *X*?

Strong
Response:
There is no conflict of interest for us. We do not solicit, and information about the prospects is not taken from one study to another. But if we cannot convince you that this is so, we would never have a comfortable relationship. Conflict of interest is in the eye of the beholder.

Weak
Response:
Of course not; don't worry about the question.

QUESTION: How can we best check your references?

Strong
Response:
Here is a list of every client we have served; feel free to check with board members and staff at all of them. You might want to ask *X* this question; we did not do so well with *Y* because. . . .

Weak
Response:
There is no need to spend time calling trustees; staff officers on the list we will send to you can give you the full story.

Comment:
Those who obfuscate, confuse, or worm their way around on this item will only cause trouble later.

QUESTION: How about travel and other costs? How will we be able to control that?

Strong
Response:
Together, we can estimate them in advance and build them into a fee—or agree not to go beyond X dollars. You will control everything; expenses will be billed separately for travel you authorize.

Weak
Response:
Don't worry, we will hold them down.

Comment:
This seemingly trivial question can be particularly important. Most firms will work with an organization to establish an interview schedule covering areas of the country where prospective donors must be seen. By retaining final control and approval, you can make certain that costs for such travel do not exceed an agreed-upon budget. Some firms approach the matter differently, estimating in advance almost all of what will be involved and adding it to the fee for conducting the study. "We can see those 60 people at a cost of x dollars. Our travel costs, except for anything over 1500 miles, will be y dollars; so your total fee, for the study, will be $x + y +$ any long distance travel." Then there is no haggling later over charges, and the firm is not burdened with extensive accounting chores.

All too often, someone on the committee will insist on asking these questions:

- Can you tell us how much you have raised for each of the institutions you have served?

- Can you apply a formula and tell us what our goal should be?

Neither question is useful. In the first instance, consultants do not raise the money. They help. Success comes when the partnership (staff, volunteers, counsel) pulls together. So the answer is simply that "institution x raised y dollars." In the second instance, one has to ask "which formula"? If all capital campaigns for construction and endowment support could reach 10 times what the same donors contribute annually, that would be a yardstick. But at some institutions the factor can easily go to 20 or more. As you will see in chapter 9, the study is needed to pinpoint a more precise figure. And we know, further, that goals cannot be projected on the basis of a school's enrollment, an agency's client roster length, or an orchestra's subscription base. Each situation is different.

ESTIMATING EXPENSES

The cost of a capital campaign is discussed in more detail in chapter 14. But a note on expenses is important here, for the fees are an important topic in the interview and will influence some of your questions. Although it is difficult, at the interview stage, for a committee to add up what the total costs will be in using consultants, here are some angles to consider.

- Who will be doing the interviewing in the precampaign study? Obviously, an experienced senior officer of a firm commands a higher fee than a junior type who has just been hired by the consulting organization.

- Does the prospect plan to offer the study as a "loss leader"— knowing that the unprofitable interviewing process will be followed by a much more profitable period when resident direction is supplied?

- Is each prospect offering the same services in a study and for campaign counseling? If it is difficult to tell, ask tough questions.

- Are the fees negotiable? Of course, but within reason. Remember that no reputable firm will charge less than what it is charging a neighboring, similar, or competing institution for the same services. If the work is reduced (by conducting, say, 50 instead of 75 interviews) you may not be economizing intelligently, as some very key prospects will not be seen. And at a reduced fee the firm may not be able to assign its best people.

Beware of bargains. As explained later, the investment in a consulting firm is relatively small—especially when your urgent objectives require such substantial giving.

CONCLUDING THE INTERVIEW

To close each interview, the chairman should explain how the committee will make its decision. Tell each prospective consultant how long the process will take. If additional written material is being requested, be sure that both parties understand when it is due and what is to be included, e.g., notes on conduct of the study, services to be offered after the study, fees and payment schedules, and background information on staff experience in similar situations.

And do not be afraid to let the candidates know how many others—and who—are being considered. If it is clear to the committee that the firm being seen is not right at all for the assignment, you should say so immediately.

Chapter 6

THE FINAL CHOICE

> *They all seem equally capable—let's just pick one and get started!*
> —Comment of a selection committee member

After the interviews, you may find that your choice is easy, that one of the candidates stands out above the others. More likely, all of the final candidates will have several good qualities to offer, making your decision a difficult one. By this time, you may have spent a couple of months narrowing the field of candidates to these final few, and it would be a mistake to jump to a quick decision based on the most recent impression from the interview. It is time, once again, to review systematically all that you know about each candidate.

THE PROCESS—A CHECKLIST

When recommending a choice to the board of trustees, the selection committee should rank each firm seen. Determining its order of preference will force the committee to weigh carefully many factors. It will be important to have notes on each interview (preferably not a tape of the discussions because the use of a recorder would have been inhibiting to both sides). A checklist for reaching a decision follows.

☐ 1. Review how the committee felt about each firm at the time of the interview and now when all of the groups have been seen.

☐ 2. Discuss the reference checks you have completed (see below).

☐ 3. Talk about the written material you requested from each firm.

☐ 4. Come to a clear understanding of fees to be charged by each firm.

☐ 5. Seek answers to questions that develop by calling the respective firms immediately.

☐ 6. Try to arrive at a consensus, not a split vote. If the committee is split, you may have difficulty instilling a sense of confidence about the campaign when you meet with the full board.

CHECKING REFERENCES

No organizations should retain a consultant without checking references carefully. After you have decided that a prospect is your first choice, ask him/her to supply:

1. A list of all clients served during the past five years.

2. The names of institutions where consulting assignments have gone well for all parties.

3. A list of institutions served two or more times by the firm.

4. Background data on a few situations where everything went wrong.

There is no need to ask for the names of specific people the consultant worked with at any of the institutions. Often, a better sense of the consultant's performance can be obtained when you call (not write) the staff and board members of another organization who are known by your own staff and board.

Raise these specific questions when checking references:

- How do those who were interviewed during a precampaign study feel about the experience? Which members of the firm were involved in the interviewing process? Was there any breach of confidentiality?

- Who from the firm worked with your organization during the campaign? Can you tell us about the strengths and weaknesses of that individual?

- What difference did it make to your organization and the campaign you completed to have the firm involved?

- Would you retain this consultant for another campaign?

- Can you comment on personal characteristics—reliability, punctuality, responsiveness in returning telephone calls?

- Were the consultant's communications skills (speaking and writing) effective?

- Do you feel that the institution received a fair return for the money invested in counsel?

There are other reference sources. If, for example, the firm has served many independent schools, it might be wise to ask the leadership of local, regional, and national associations to comment. That way you can gain a perspective on the firm's conduct of its work for similar institutions. Talking with a few individuals who have been interviewed by firm members in a precampaign study should also prove particularly revealing. Other types of firms involved with organizations (printers, graphic designers, lawyers, and accountants) often have an interesting perspective because they have seen so many different fund-raising consultants at work for various institutions.

NOTIFYING PROSPECTS OF THE FINAL DECISION

The standard wisdom is that good news comes by telephone and bad news is delivered in the mail. An organization can build much good will for itself by calling all of the competitors by telephone just as soon as a decision has been made. A firm you turn down today may be the one you need several years later. Everyone benefits when you tell the losers what impressed you about their presentations but why you still chose another firm. Open communication of this type is much more valuable than simply writing "thanks-but-no-thanks" letters to the losers a month after the decision has been made.

Chapter 7

THE AGREEMENT— SIGNING ON THE DOTTED LINE

Your long, hard efforts, which may have taken two or three months, have paid off. You have found the consultant you want and have reached an agreement on the task to be done. Likely, one of the reasons you chose the consultant is that the person or firm seems reliable and trustworthy—so much so that you might be tempted to say, "We don't need a formal contract. A simple handshake will do." The problem with accepting anyone's "word," of course, is that verbal agreements can not be enforced should they need to be; a contract can help to protect you against dishonesty or malpractice. But that is not likely to occur, especially if you have carefully chosen a reputable consultant. The real problem is that the substance of an oral agreement can easily be misunderstood and misinterpreted. Despite the best of intentions on both sides, disagreements about the task to be completed can develop, particularly if results turn out to be less than anticipated or the campaign is longer than planned.

A written agreement solves most problems in this area. Many states require a fund-raising consultant to file copies of all contracts with the attorney general or consumer protection department. But whether required by law or not, it makes sense to have a document which will serve to avoid disagreements later on. The contract can take one of several forms:

- A simple letter, drafted by the consultant, signed by the consultant and the gift-supported organization's authorized officer.

- The consultant's proposal, adjusted to reflect modifications in the work to be performed after discussions about the assignment have been completed (again, signed by both parties).

- A formal contract, based on the consultant's proposal to the organization, which spells out the specific details of the assignment and is signed by both parties.

POINTS TO CONSIDER

No matter what its form, a contract should include a number of standard items:

1. The purpose of the consulting assignment: precampaign study to determine how much money can be raised and how a drive should be organized; counseling for a campaign or a direct mail program; or, perhaps, just an internal audit of the development function.

2. Methodology to be used—for example, a study posing specific questions to 60 potential donors.

3. The product to be delivered to the organization—from a comprehensive *written* report on the precampaign study with findings, conclusions, and recommendations to an *oral* report which encompasses recommendations only for a new internal arrangement of the development office.

4. A statement about fees and expenses, and when payments are to be made.

5. A provision stating when the assignment is to begin and how long it will take to complete.

6. A clear indication of which of a firm's personnel will be involved in carrying out the assignment.

7. A statement indicating how, and under what conditions, either party can terminate the agreement.

An effective contract, properly drawn, eliminates misunderstandings and provides a series of benchmarks to be used by both the consultant and the organization when assessing progress. In fact, a properly worded agreement, fully understood by both parties, is usually not referred to again in the course of an assignment. Everyone knows what is expected.

SAMPLE AGREEMENT AND COMMENT

In the following sample contract form, a consulting firm's proposal has been turned into a contract. Comments about the meaning and importance of each section have been added in boldface. (NOTE: As with any legal proceeding, you should have your agreement reviewed by professional legal counsel. This contract, indeed this chapter, is presented for discussion purposes only and not intended for actual use as presented.)

SAMPLE CONTRACT

Proposal/Agreement

(name and address of hiring organization)

and

(name and address of consultant)

I. EXECUTIVE SUMMARY AND INTRODUCTION

This Proposal/Agreement confirms the decision of the organization to retain the Firm of (name, place or headquarters) for a 90-day period, commencing when the document is signed by both parties, to carry out a three-part study designed to assess the leadership and donor potential for a $5,000,000 capital campaign. Components include: (1) development of a brief mini-case statement explaining what the task is and why the funds are needed to complete it; (2) testing that case in a series of 75 interviews with prospective donors; and (3) providing the framework in which the strategy, structure, systems, and staffing pattern for a campaign can be placed.

At the end of the 90-day period the Firm will submit a comprehensive, written report to the (organization) which presents our findings, conclusions, and recommendations. Specifically, this document will cover:

(1) how much of the $5,000,000 objective will be available within a two-year period;
(2) how much it will cost to raise;
(3) the strategy (plan) for the campaign;
(4) the organizational committee structure required;
(5) the timetable needed;
(6) systems, staffing, and volunteer leadership suggested for the programs;
(7) role, if any, for fund-raising counsel (as well as projected costs); and
(8) description of the steps to be taken in starting the effort to obtain significant capital support.

When the Report is submitted, it will be acompanied by:

(1) an outline of the "case for support";
(2) recommendations for those to serve on a 10-15 member Executive Campaign Steering Committee (ECSC);
(3) materials for counsel's use in preparing Committee members to solicit effectively; and
(4) a complete, confidential analysis of the interviews indicating which prospects should be seen by which solicitor—and asked for how much money toward which of the goal's components to be orally presented to campaign's leadership.

The Firm will also be asked to coordinate and direct the activities of other consultants who may be asked to complete such tasks as:

(1) direct mail program to prospects at lower levels (dollar potential);
(2) publications;
(3) staff executive search (if needed); and
(4) data systems design.

The 90-day study period fee will be $XX,XXX, inclusive of all out-of-pocket expenses for travel and associated costs. Both parties will reserve the right to terminate the project after the initial 25 interviews have been completed if responses have indicated that it is not worthwhile to finish the assignment. In this case the total fee will be reduced to $XX,XXX. Toward the end of the 90-day period the Firm will be prepared to recommend how it might be involved in helping to implement campaign plans (and at what cost). Any and all arrangements entered into by the parties can be terminated at any point by the (organization).

> **Comment: Although there is no requirement to do so, it is often helpful to summarize the entire contract in several paragraphs so that busy executives serving on on a board can get the gist of the document quickly and leave knit-picking to others.**

II. THE THREE-PART STUDY

A. *Developing the Case Statement*

Working with staff, and drawing on various (organization) planning documents, the Firm will prepare a brief statement which sets forth:

(1) where the (organization) is headed;
(2) what specific costs are involved in reaching its goals; and
(3) what difference the capital support being discussed will make in the quality of the institution.

B. *Testing the Case*

The Firm will then take this preliminary statement to 75 confidential, in-depth interviews with individuals across the country (including trustees, alumni, parents, and friends) and will raise these questions:

1. Reaction to the statement in terms of its importance to the (organization) and its objectives for the future.

2. Sources of support available, and at approximately what levels, from individuals, foundations, and corporations.

3. Individuals who should be in position to provide the type of fund-raising leadership required for the task.

4. Components of the plan (goals) with the most appeal.

5. Ways in which the story should be told.

6. Personal willingness to be involved in asking others (individuals, foundations, and corporations) to participate.

7. Willingness to support the program (personally, company, foundation).

C. Strategy, Structure, Systems, Staffing

On the basis of what is learned during the early interviews, the Firm will begin to develop a comprehensive campaign plan. Those sections dealing with structure, systems, and staffing will be reviewed with the (organization) before the Report is submitted.

Comment: In this way you will be prepared to move forward with the campaign just as soon as the formal document is submitted to, and accepted by, the Board of Trustees (assuming that the recommendations are positive).

The Firm will be dealing with the following matters as the interviewing process continues during the study period:

(1) data base for reviewing past support and keeping track of new prospect and donors from this time forward;
(2) prospect research;
(3) direct mail program (initial sampling);
(4) office organization and equipment required;
(5) staff functions to be filled for a campaign; and
(6) refinement of the preliminary case statement.

In mid-September, at the study's conclusion, the Firm will submit a comprehensive, written report to the (organization) which presents findings, conclusions, and recommendations in as specific a form as possible for implementing campaign plans.

Comment: When the methodology to be used has been spelled out in such detail, there is little room for confusion about what services are to be performed. Also, this section has the advantage of linking the methodology to the product (report), making the approach that much easier to understand. But there is one danger to this style of drafting: No room is left for flexibility and adjustment if it takes a bit longer to complete one aspect of the project or another through no real fault on the part of either party.

III. THE FIRM'S PARTICIPATION

(Name), President of the Firm (or other official as applicable), will conduct more than 30 of the confidential interviews, including as many of the Trustees and key prospects as possible in the study, and will be involved in all other aspects of the assignment. (Name), Vice-President, will complete the other interviews and share in the balance of the assignment; the (organization) will interview (name) before we agree to have her participate in the project. (President's name) has headed the Firm for twelve years and has been involved in designing more than 100 capital campaigns. He is a graduate of Dartmouth College, lives in Manhattan, and served as a Vice-President of both Wheaton College and The New School, as well as special assistant to the president at Sarah Lawrence College, before founding the company. (Vice-President's name) lives in Bennington, Vermont, and has been involved with the Firm for nearly a decade. A graduate of Radcliffe College, she has completed studies and implemented campaign plans for such organizations as The Metropolitan Opera, Whitney Museum, New York City Ballet, South Street Seaport, and Buffalo Philharmonic.

Comment: No question remains about who will be doing the work for the organization in the firm's behalf. At this point there can be no hedging by the consultant, such as "subject to availability." The background information supplied will also answer questions about capability from those unable to meet the consultant before agreement signing.

IV. BEYOND THE STUDY

If the study's results are positive, it is anticipated that the Firm will be retained to provide continuing assistance in the implementation of all campaign plans. However, neither party would be making a commitment at this time to any arrangements beyond the 90-day study. If the Firm is asked to offer campaign services later, a second contract will be negotiated and will include the following tasks to be carried out during a 12- to 15-month counseling period:

1. completion of the comprehensive case statement (building from the expanded outline started during the study and including much of the data gathered during the interviews);

2. organization of the 10- to 15-member Executive Campaign Steering Committee (based, again, on what has been learned during the study period);

3. planning for, and participation in, all monthly meetings of the Committee;

4. training of all volunteers, beginning with the Committee, in solicitation techniques (using material developed during the study);

5. training of staff;

6. development of all campaign literature (copy)—based on the case statement;

7. coordination and direction for all other consultants involved—from direct mail to executive search (if that is necessary), data base management and publications design;

8. rating and assignment of campaign prospects (on the basis of interview results);

9. weekly meetings with the staff and Committee leadership;

10. preparation of budgets, timetables, and implementation calendars (all based on preliminary projections submitted in the study report); and

11. monitoring of progress toward all agreed upon objectives (how much money from whom and by when).

Comment: While it is not necessary to describe what might happen after a study in this agreement for a precampaign project, most organizations appreciate having some specific reference to the program which will follow a study if the results are positive.

V. ASSESSING PROGRESS

After the initial 25 interviews in the study have been completed, counsel will meet with the (organization) staff to review progress and assess results without violating the confidential aspects of the individual sessions. Information about the interviews will be shared with you at that time, as well as at the study's conclusion, so that the (organization) will have a clear picture of its leadership and donor potential. Some vital information about which solicitors should call on which prospects will be communicated to you outside the study report—but to preserve confidentiality no attributions will be made.

If the Firm is retained to provide assistance during the campaign, monthly progress reviews will be conducted against benchmarks previously established. The (organization) will reserve the right to terminate any and all arrangements with the Firm after notice has been given (30 days is customary).

Comment: While most studies can and should proceed without interruption, there are situations in which the consultant can provide reassurance to a skeptical board that not a bit of work more than necessary will be undertaken and that progress will be assessed in a regular and systematic fashion.

VI. FEE

The Firm's comprehensive fee for the 90-day study will be $XX,XXX, inclusive of all out-of-pocket expenses for travel and related costs. There will be no further charge to the (organization) for services rendered during this three-month segment. An initial payment of $XX,XXX will be expected when the Agreement is signed by both parties; $XX,XXX more will be due 30 days later;

$X,XXX will be payable 30 days after that; and the balance ($ X,XXX) will be payable 30 days after that. In the event that the study is terminated after the initial 25 interviews, the total fee will be reduced to $XX,XXX. It is anticipated that there will be one trip for interviewing purposes to (place) and to the (place).

> **Comment: Of course many firms will separate the fee from expenses and will suggest a "cap" beyond which it won't go in travel and related costs without the written concurrence of the organization. It is essential to have some description (and limit) on the expense side to avoid disagreements later. When a firm inlcudes travel costs in its comprehensive fee, the organization should take note of that when it attempts to compare charges various firms might ask for in their proposals.**

> **The timing of payments can be based on time elapsed or on the portions of the work completed; the gift-supported organization can plan its finances and cash/flow when it knows, in advance, what its commitment wlll be (and when payments are due).**

> **Both parties need an "out" clause; no self-respecting consultant will want to go forward with a study in which initial results have been overwhelmingly negative. Knowing that additonal interviews cannot appreciably alter what has already been learned, the consultant should make a recommendation to terminate the project--and then advise the organization on ways to mend fences, make a stronger case, or proceed in other ways to educate and cultivate a constituency before a major campaign is initiated. The consultant has a reputation to protect, and an organization served fairly will speak well of the outsider who stopped the meter early and will probably want this consultant to serve when conditions have improved.**

If counseling continues under a second Agreement, the fee schedule should run to no more than:

1. four months @ $X,XXX = $XX,XXX

2. four months @ $X,XXX = $XX,XXX

3. four months @ $X,XXX = $XX,XXX

4. all additional months @ $X,XXX = . . .

Comment: When an organization has such a clear-cut indication of potential campaign counseling charges so early on, no one will be surprised when the study is completed and discussions begin about the cost of continuing counseling for the drive.

The terms of this Agreement will go into effect as soon as both parties have signed the document.

Accepted by:

For the (organization name)

_____   _____   _____
Signature   Title   Date

For the Firm

_____   _____
(Name) President   Date

★★★★★

In the final analysis, a "good" contract hardly assures an effective counseling program. Allowance must be made for the unexpected, particularly in a precampaign study. A measure of good will is needed on both sides to get by the normal difficulties in scheduling interview appointments.

A well-drawn contract, however, is the starting point for a relationship that is productive and rewarding for all concerned. Knowing what to expect is the key; well-informed clients are always more sympathetic and understanding if problems develop later.

Chapter 8

ADDRESSING SPECIAL NEEDS

No problem! Whatever you need, we can do!
—Sometimes famous last words

When you retain a firm to guide a capital campaign, additional assistance may still be needed from specialists on a variety of needs. In interviews with consultants, your selection committee should be able to define those requirements and ascertain whether the firm can supply them or if additional help should be sought. A word of caution: Beware of the consultant who insists that "we can take care of whatever comes up." No one can be a specialist in everything. While the primary consultant should focus on central issues, there will be a number of special fund-raising matters that require the best thinking obtainable. Some of these special services are covered below.

SPECIALIZED CONSULTING SERVICES

Executive Search

Several of the major consulting firms have their own executive search offices guided by senior officers who devote full attention to finding development professionals for the staffs of gift-supported organizations. Even organizations using another firm for campaign counseling can use this executive-search service. A few executive-search consultants have now established their own practices specializing in gift-supported institutions and focusing on fund raising, and a number of the general search firms with offices in several cities have special divisions to meet the needs of gift-supported organizations.

Most fund-raising firms will agree to conduct searches as part of their counseling assignment, but you should remember that this might not be a specialty. If they cannot find the right candidate quickly, precious time will be wasted, and you should move quickly to the professional search track—even if the cost will come to 25 percent or more of an initial year's salary for a top-flight development officer (really a modest investment when the fund-raising stakes are considered).

Publications

Although a number of fund-raising consulting firms maintain their own departments for the writing, design, and production of brochures and collateral material (from pledge cards and letterhead to newsletters and forms), most organizations have relationships with local companies that specialize in use of the printed word. A decision must be made quickly about the approach to be taken. If a consulting firm confines its services to capital campaign direction, its representatives should still develop the basic copy for a case statement, which will ultimately become the campaign brochure, because these consultants have learned from their interviews precisely how the fund-raising message should be conveyed.

It is crucial that all other consultants used by an institution recognize that the firm engaged for fund-raising counseling be in charge—in effect, to serve as lead counsel; otherwise, the organization runs the risk of publications being out of sync with the campaign's objectives, or, in the case of an executive search, the wrong development officer being hired for the task.

A consultant's experience. One low-profile college in Rochester, New York, had engaged our firm to provide consulting services for a capital campaign—but first to assist in completing the search for a media consultant who could help the institution become more visible. The firm chosen for the assignment learned in a study of its own that few community opinion leaders knew very much about the college. The publicity campaign that followed was a model of its type, using television spots, newspaper ads, publicity, targeted mailings, and speeches to increase awareness of the institution. We began our precampaign study in a much-improved environment, until the day when someone got the idea that billboards were needed by the admissions officers for their recruitment efforts. From what the media consultants and our firm had already uncovered, it was clear that this approach would be useful in admissions but would destroy all of the links established to opinion leaders and the major donor prospects now identified. Our "awareness" effort had done its job in a low-key professional way; a louder technique was inappropriate. Because our firm was "lead counsel," we were looked to by the entire staff and all other consultants involved for direction on the issue, and the billboard concept was quickly shelved.

Planned Giving

As tax laws become more complex, most institutions need guidance in how prospects should be given information on a variety of matters related to personal financial planning techniques and approaches, ranging from wills and gifts of life insurance to the much more esoteric instruments that return to donors (and often their heirs) income for life. Although some firms have specialists in this area, most do not. Quite often, an organization will want to retain a special consultant to explain planned giving to the board and others, and even to join volunteer solicitors on calls when technical information is needed by the prospective donors.

A consultant's experience. We have assisted in selection of these experts and have worked in tandem with them. In a college situation we have run joint training seminars for the volunteer solicitors. Our firm would take the participants through role-playing calls on prospects, ending with the would-be donors saying, "But we cannot do it right now." The planned-giving expert then continued the dramatization, having the solicitors explain to the prospects how they might take advantage of long-term giving techniques. Thus the volunteers felt they had an extra arrow in their quivers when it seemed difficult to obtain an outright commitment.

Data Processing

With technological advances taking place seemingly weekly, no fund-raising consultant can really offer state-of-the-art advice in the organization of information systems. Again, specialists are needed. Some confine their practices to the gift-supported sector and have developed their own software (the programs that tell the computers what you want done with your data and then do it), which can be tailored to the specific needs of an institution.

Beware of quick fixes. It is an arduous task to develop the right information system for an organization, and the computer will not solve all fund-raising problems. It is just a tool to do a job more efficiently. Beware, too, of a solution that ties all departments of an institution together; it may sound economical and reasonable, but much will be lost if the development office is left with the lowest priority and has no free-standing equipment on which to deal with its most urgent problems. Try to picture the board chairman who wants a printout of all $100,000 prospects in Chicago for a trip he is planning and has to be told that another office has priority to complete its inventory of institutional widgets. A good systems consultant can avoid this trap.

Direct Mail and Telemarketing

In an annual giving program, direct mail will be an important element in success or failure. Many specialists can help organizations plan their programs in such a way that proven techniques are applied (covering such things as sample or test mailings to length of letter, how it is signed, and when it is mailed). Telemarketing (also known as telefundraising) is a relatively new concept employed toward the end of a capital campaign. Those prospects who were not seen earlier in person are reached by well-trained telephone callers (not your own volunteers, usually). Most consulting firms are not equipped to provide this service. Clearly, experts are needed for this task, but few firms have this capability.

You should expect your campaign consultant to suggest that others be brought in to help on a project; the work of the additional consultants will complement the primary consultant, enabling the campaign to reach many who would otherwise not participate.

Part III
Working With the
Consultant

Part III is a lengthy survey of the work between you and the consultant during the stages of a capital campaign. The foundation of the drive is the precampaign study, which tests the possibilities of success. Everything in the ensuing drive is based on that feasibility study. The stages of the campaign are carefully unfolded, from the initial nucleus fund to the final phases. Attention is paid to potential problems in campaign organization, training staff and solicitors, and monitoring results along the way. A frank discussion is included on the pitfalls and opportunities of the consultant's relationship with your organization's staff and executives.

Chapter 9

THE PRECAMPAIGN STUDY—ASSESSING PHILANTHROPIC CLIMATE

There's plenty of money out there—we don't need a study, all we have to do is ask.
—Comment of a board member

All too often, a consulting firm hears the kind of message that confirms the importance of the precampaign study. Ironically, the message will come from the board chairman of an institution and sound like this: "We already know everything about our prospects—who they are, what they will give, and which solicitor should call on specific people. Why do we have to waste time on a study? We only want your advice on running the campaign." Upon hearing that message, a consultant knows, first, that the organization has probably identified only half of its possible donors. Furthermore, the board chairman's certainty about "what they will give" is most likely based on what donors have contributed to past drives and makes no provision for either the new campaign's urgency or a change in prospects' philanthropic interests or finances. Finally, judgments about which solicitor should approach which prospect may be based solely on presumed friendship.

The board chairman's off-the-cuff analysis would suffice if a campaign could be run solely on instinct and common sense. But experience shows that better data is required. As stressed in chapter 2, the precampaign study provides the information and projections that are the essential foundation of a successful campaign.

THE FEASIBILITY STUDY—WHY?

The precampaign study tests the feasibility of a capital campaign by answering these questions:

1. Is your case compelling and urgent?

2. Is leadership available to organize the drive and ask for support?

3. Will specific donor prospects give at the high levels required for success?

4. Is there strong interest in the planned drive's various objectives (automation for a library, a scholarship endowment for a school, or office renovation for a health agency)?

5. Is the climate right, considering competing campaigns, economic conditions, and the date of the organization's last fund-raising program?

In sum: Is the goal attainable?

Purpose of the Study Interviews

The study is founded on confidential, in-person interviews conducted by counsel with a number (almost always more than 25 and usually less than 100) of an organization's board members, major past donors, current prospects, and opinion leaders. Even a few dissidents, who are critical of the organization, will be interviewed. From an analysis of the interviews, counsel can reach conclusions and make specific recommendations for the conduct of a fundraising program. Simultaneously with the confidential interviews, counsel conducts an "audit" of an organization, consisting of a records review within the organization and sessions with members of the staff. This audit provides information on an organization's readiness for a major campaign. Counsel learns which systems and procedures must be adjusted, what new staff members are needed, how prospect research should be conducted, and how much capability already exists for giving internal leadership to the proposed drive.

If a study could prove that a campaign is feasible, therefore enabling the consultants to develop guideposts for conducting the program, why is a structured fund-raising program really necessary? The answer is both simple and complex. Basically, the study—as well as fund raising in general—is an art, not a science. The consultant's experienced ear picks up signals, not conclusive facts. A prospective donor might say: "The program appeals to me, but I'm far from certain how our family will respond this time. When you are ready to call on us, I hope that Harry won't be given the assignment." Counsel's interpretation of such a response could be that the case is probably compelling but not yet urgent for that prospect; that the donor leans toward doing considerably more than was contributed in the last drive; that several family members will be in on the decision; or that the right solicitor has not been identified yet. Further probing will determine who solicitor X should be.

How Long Should the Study Take?

A feasibility study often takes three months to complete. It can take far less time, especially if it is being conducted on behalf of a small-town church or local youth group (for which interviewees are local). But if your constituents are scattered and diverse, you must allow several months.

The consultant should not conduct more than four interviews per day for any one organization; otherwise, experience has shown, it becomes hard to listen carefully. Nor should the consultants be interviewing every day for the same organization; perspective can be lost quickly. You will find that additional interviews need to be scheduled toward the end of the study with individuals whose names do not surface until they are mentioned during the first sessions in a study. Some "soak time" is needed for those who have been interviewed to consider how they feel deep-down about the plans and to talk them over with others. Similarly, the consultant needs a period of reflection to sift the data. If something turns out to be wrong in the interview format, there is time to make adjustments. Finally, if the initial interviews bring internal problems to the surface (ranging from substantive issues to practical problems such as how rapidly gift receipts are mailed), there is enough time during a three-month study to correct those practices prior to the submission of a study report.

If the study's results are positive, it makes little sense to delay the start of a campaign. Data gathered in the study will rapidly go out of date. The best prospects are ready to give, and if the program is not initiated, they will focus their attention on other interests. A three-month study period, including the internal audit, is adequate for most organizations to prepare for the launching of a major fund-raising effort.

The Link of Planning to the Campaign

The study is a useful bridge to link the precampaign planning process to the campaign itself. After completing long-range planning for a capital campaign (see chapter 3), the board is likely to feel that its constituents will agree with the preliminary objectives. Unfortunately, not all of the institution's friends will read and understand the material, recognize the financial implications for those who believe in the cause, or sense the urgency of the situation.

The interviews by counsel keep many of the principal prospects in touch with the proposed campaign objectives. Prospective donors feel pleased that their advice is being requested, having been told that the planning process will not be complete until their opinions have been considered. The interviews telegraph to constituents that a drive will follow and that the organization is preparing for it in a professional way. By conducting a study, you are taking into account the feelings of a larger group than just a committee or a board; thus the campaign's message about an institution's needs will be less what its leadership wants to say and more what the prospects might want to hear.

ORGANIZING THE STUDY

There is no single way to develop and manage the study. What follows is a fairly typical approach.

The Interview Selection Committee—Guiding the Process

It is helpful if the selection committee that chose the consultant, or another small ad hoc group (five would be the ideal size), works with counsel on all aspects of the study. It should be understood that this group will go out of business when the study report is presented.

Compiling the Interview Sample

The list of persons to be interviewed should be completed by the committee and counsel together. The general list of names should be broken down into categories. For a typical organization, the categories might look like this:

- all donors of $10,000 or more to the most recent campaign

- anyone who has given $1,000 or more to the annual fund at any time during the past three years

- at least ten prospective donors of major gifts who have not yet contributed significantly to this organization

- a handful of "dissidents" who are inclined to be pessimistic about fund raising

- all Board members

- several past Board members

- several opinion leaders (respected citizens who know the organization but are not potential donors)

These categories could produce as many as 150 prospective interviewees for a typical organization. If it has been agreed that 50 individuals are to be interviewed, it will be necessary to prune the roster. In the pruning, however, no board member should be eliminated.

If the list can be cut to 75, you will have just about the right number. A few will decline to be interviewed for reasons of illness, age, or change of interest. Others will be traveling on business or otherwise unavailable. If a large number of the best prospects decline to be interviewed, a sign is being given that this is not the right moment for a campaign. This rarely happens. People like to share their feelings and offer opinions. Turn-downs are more likely to be attributed to an inadequate letter requesting the interview or poor follow-up by the organization in setting an appointment date.

The need for objectivity: a consultant's experience. A distinguished group of oncologists once called on our firm to review a study report which they had received from financial consultants (not experienced fund-raising counsel) about the feasibility of an endowment drive to support a major cancer research program. The physicians were dismayed about the report because the interview sample had included 80 fellow doctors, all of whom reported that the program was invaluable and that funds should be sought for it. When I reviewed the report, I had to say it reminded me of the statement attributed to Willie Sutton: "You rob banks because that's where the money is." And I went on to explain to the doctors that any effective study would have to encompass interviews with individuals, companies, and foundations in a position to make large gifts. "To help you in this situation, we would want to conduct a second study focusing on confidential interviews with wealthy patients and their families—not the oncologists."

This seemed to be an acceptable approach until they asked how I proposed to obtain the names of those we should see. When I suggested that they themselves would have to ask the prospective interviewees to meet with counsel, the meeting almost came to an abrupt end. "Do you mean, Mr. Raybin," one physician asked "That you would ask us to violate the confidential patient-physician relationship in the interest of obtaining money for our research?"

"Precisely so," I replied. The pained looks indicated an obvious conflict. Funds were needed to carry on the research in behalf of the afflicted patients who were in a position to provide financial help for a program in their own interest. But their physicians were not willing to breach the relationship in an effort to achieve funding for the project. Sensing that no further discussion would resolve this issue, I asked for a week to develop a letter that would deal with all sides of this problem and be an acceptable piece for the physicians to send to their patients. Everyone was skeptical, but agreed to the delay.

My draft letter was similar in tone and style to our usual approach. But we added a few points: 1) you (the patient or family member) might not know of my (the physician's) involvement with the research program; 2) here is what we do and have achieved so far; 3) we need help to continue what we are doing, and I would like to *give you an opportunity to participate* if you would like to do so—beginning with the interview our consultants are conducting in the program's behalf.

That did it. At our next meeting, after the draft letter had been circulated, each of the seven key physicians brought lists and lists of those who might be interviewed. In the following days they rewrote the letter to present even more compelling reasons why the prospective interviewee should meet with the consultants.

When I asked the organization's president why there had been such a turn-around in the group's thinking, he said: "We agreed with you that we were only giving our patients and their loved ones an *opportunity* to be included *if they felt up to doing so*—with no real pressure from any of us. Beyond that, we had probably been negligent in not telling them previously about the program and the results which have been important to them. Finally, what we are doing is so important that we can't be constrained by our feelings, and the risk of offending anyone is small given the way in which the letters are being written."

Writing the Interview Request Letter

A letter should be prepared to explain the study process and to describe how the interviews will be conducted. The board chairperson, unless not well-known by the constituents, should sign the letter. If the president, headmaster, or executive director *only* of an organization signs the letter, the proposed drive will be viewed as "his/her campaign," and the enlistment of volunteer leadership will be more difficult. ("If the paid leaders feel so strongly about it, let them raise the money.") For similar reasons, the development officer is also the wrong person to sign the letter. The letter should make several points:

1. The organization really wants guidance and advice.

2. The interview will *not* be a solicitation.

3. Specific questions will be raised by our consultants. (Name the subjects.)

4. The interview will be confidential.

5. Appointments will be made in the following way. (Describe how.)

6. The interview will take no longer than 45 minutes.

7. You will be interviewed by (person) of (firm), which our Board has retained for this purpose.

8. The firm has conducted similar studies for several organizations. (Name them.)

9. Close with a sentence stating, in effect, "My office will be calling you in the next few weeks to make an appointment for our consultant to meet with you."

A sample letter appears in figure 9-1.

Planning the Interview

There are as many types of interview formats as there are consultants. Whatever the format, it is essential that the meetings be conducted as dialogues, not methodical question-and-answer checklists. But a standard series of questions must be used in the study. An experienced consultant knows how to adapt the format so that all of those seen are asked the same questions, even if the sequence is adjusted; that the interviewee feels that the session was more than polite conversation; that no important material is skipped; and that the interviewee recognizes that all areas mentioned in the letter were dealt with thoroughly. A sample interview format appears in figure 9-2.

Making the Interview Appointments

As mentioned earlier, the request letter should close with a sentence saying something to this effect: "My office will be calling you in the next few weeks to make an appointment for our consultant to meet with you." Then the development officer, or another senior staff member who understands the process and knows the constituency, calls each prospective interviewee directly to make appointments for the consultants. The consultant will set aside blocks of time for this purpose. Using this procedure allows the development officer to become better known to important individuals. Many of those who received the letter will not bother reading it or will need clarification, and during this call the staff officer can explain why the study is being undertaken and why it is important for the letter's recipient to participate. This call can also reassure interviewees that the sessions will be confidential, that no gift will be solicited, and that the consultants are qualified and suitable for this task. Moreover, many of those being called will have other questions on their minds apart from the study; the telephone conversation is a fine chance for dialogue at another level.

If, instead, the consultants arrange their own appointments, much can go wrong. If a prospective interviewee says "no," it is difficult for a relative stranger to be persuasive about why the answer should be "yes." An unknown consultant becomes nothing more than a salesperson or poll-taker in the mind of a prospective interviewee.

Arranging interviews can take as many as 325 telephone calls to make 50 appointments; the staff time involved is an important investment and is as much a part of the study process as the interviews themselves. Setting the stage for the consultants is vital. A suggested approach to the making of appointments appears in figure 9-3.

FIG. 9-1: Sample precampaign study interview request letter

Dear _____:

When the (college) was created in the middle-1960's, it would have been difficult to predict that its aspirations to become a premier undergraduate institution with a focus on the sciences could be fulfilled. As the institution matures in a more difficult economic era, it must now be concerned with such new issues as: 1) making science an integral part of the total curriculum; 2) widening access to higher education for both young and older adult students in the area; 3) refining its curriculum for greater depth and focus in science; and 4) integrating the college and the community in a closer public service partnership with a scientific emphasis.

Federal and state support for the college has been reduced substantially during the past several years. Private support will be needed to maintain and extend the college's unique role in science. The college's foundation, through which important funds for the institution are channeled in gifts from individuals, corporations, and foundation, has been considering a long-range development plan which will encourage friends of the institution to provide significant capital support for vital programs in the years ahead.

Before the plan is completed, the foundation would like very much to have the advice and guidance of those in the community who know the college well or have opinions and comments to offer about educational, financial, and community service priorities for the institution.

We are asking you to be one of 70 individuals who will take part in a study conducted for us by (consultant name, place of headquarters). This firm has carried out similar studies for the Metropolitan Opera, Whitney Museum, South Street Seaport, Rye Country Day School, and Greenwich Country Day School. We will call you in the next few weeks to find out when you might be able to meet for just 45 minutes with either (name) or (name) of the firm. The session can be scheduled at your convenience, and all responses will remain confidential. Our consultants will only be reporting to the foundation on the over-all pattern of response. You will be asked direct questions about: 1) how well the College is fulfilling its mission; 2) your participation in programs and events at the College; 3) areas of community service in need of further attention; 4) reaction to a preliminary list of educational and financial priorities; 5) suggestions for leadership of a development program; 6) comments on sources of support within the community; and 7) your own interest in specific areas and willingness to participate in a program providing support for them.

The interview *is not* a solicitation for funds; we simply need your counsel before we take another step in our planning process. Thank you, in advance, for your willingness to participate in the study.

Sincerely,

FIG. 9-2: Sample precampaign study interview outline for prospective college campaign

I. Introduction
- Who we are and what we have been asked to do
- Review of letter received
- Confidentiality
- Concerned with the over-all pattern of response
- Results to be shared
- Feel free to comment beyond the scope of questions raised

II. The College
- Knowledge of the College
  —educational programs
  —other programs and projects
- Quality of the programs
- Over-all quality of the institution
- Leadership and management
- Public image

III. Case
- List of preliminary objectives
- Comments on priorities
- Specific interests and concerns
- What will be of most interest to others
- Anything not essential?
- Additions
- How the story should be conveyed

IV. Leadership
- Who will be effective in telling the College's story—and in asking for support
- Who would be helpful in leading/organizing such an effort
- Your willingness to help

V. Donors
- Who could give to such a program

	$1,000,000	$100,000	$25,000
People			
Companies			
Foundations			

- Personal interest in helping?
- Others interested in specific areas?
- Climate, competition, timing

VI. Summary and Public Relations
- Review of interview
- Again, confidentiality assured
- We will write to confirm interview; call or write back with additional comments
- College's communication with the community and with you
- Effectiveness of publications
- "One wish for or about the college"
- Thank you

FIG. 9-3: Making interview appointments — guidelines from consultant to client

Interviews are the essential source of information from which the findings, conclusions, and recommendations in our precampaign study for (organization) will be drawn. Our "rule of thumb" is four interviews per day, although we can conduct more if necessary.

We want to conduct all of the sessions in person. Telephone interviews simply do not work very well.

It is our responsibility to:

- Assign available days to you.
- Send follow-up letters to all persons seen with copies to you confirming that the interviews were completed.

It is your responsibility to:

- Draw up the interviewee listing (as we work it out with you).
- Send interview request letters.
- Follow up with telephone calls to set the specific time and place for each appointment.
- Confirm appointments by letter, card, or telephone call.
- Notify us of interview schedules in time to make travel arrangements. When a day assigned for the project cannot be used, to notify us in time to schedule other business activities.
- Make sure it is clear both to us and to those to be interviewed where the interviews are to take place.
- Schedule appointments within the allotted time frame.
- Give us listings for each day's schedule (names, addresses, hours) along with a street guide with driving directions sketched in.

The following suggestions should help you to carry through your telephone calls, in the form of some things to remember to say.

- "It will only take 30 to 45 minutes..."

- "We *need* your opinions before moving ahead with our planning process..."

- "It's strictly confidential..."

- "You'll enjoy meeting (name) of (name of firm). The firm has completed similar studies for the Metropolitan Opera, Whitney Museum, Rye Country Day School, South Street Seaport, and Columbia University."

- "Unfortunately, interviewing doesn't work well by telephone." (If pressed on this point.)

- "You can have your choice of _____, _____ or _____; if none work, I'll call back with other possibilities...or ask (name) to call you." (last resort)

WHAT NOT TO TELL THE CONSULTANT

You might feel a need to brief the consultant about each person to be seen. Nothing could be more harmful. If counsel has been told what to expect, it becomes difficult to listen objectively. Quite often, your information will be incorrect or dated. The consultant needs to be able to say, at the outset of interviews, "On purpose, we have asked the organization not to tell us anything about those being seen. We want to hear it all from you." This almost always leads to a story of how the interviewee became involved with the cause, and having that story told by the individual prospect is important. Subtle nuances guide the remaining aspects of the interview. Often, a sophisticated interviewee will say, "Of course, you know what my giving record has been." Here, too, it is nice to be able to say, "No, we don't—please tell us about it if you would like to." The reasons are more important than the dollar figures in predicting what might be expected as a pledge.

There is a conflicting school of thought and some consultants insist on being fully briefed on the backgrounds of the interviewees before the study is initiated. These consultants feel that they are more effective when they know, say, the circumstances surrounding the dismissal of a child from a school before the parents are interviewed.

THE CONFIDENTIAL INTERVIEWS—WHAT REALLY TAKES PLACE

As is often the case in fund raising, the process is at least as important as the substance. If the interviews are not pleasant experiences, a great deal can be lost for the organization. A cold, objective consultant conveys a wrong message about the planning procedures and the campaign to follow. If the consultant attempts to sell the program, sophisticated interviewees will wonder why they have agreed to be seen. A careful balance is needed. Of course, the consultants can answer questions about the organization, but his or her knowledge will be limited. In fact, if the consultant knows too much, the interview can easily fall apart and dissolve into a discussion of matters that are irrelevant to the study. An experienced consultant can and should react in these ways to the typical comments.

"I am not happy with college counseling at the school."
- This interview is confidential, as you know, but we will include your feelings, without attribution, in our report. It would be helpful to the school, however, if you would discuss the matter directly with the headmaster.

"We've done enough for the disadvantaged; this campaign should stress other objectives."
- Others we have seen have similar feelings. We will include this perspective in our report—without attribution. (Woe be unto the consultants who feel compelled to "educate" or pick fights with interviewees.)

"If Harry solicits me again, I will scream; he thinks he is so darn effective, but I just don't like him. Send someone else and I will give twice as much."
- Thanks for the tip; we won't mention it in our report, and your comment will never be attributed to you. In the course of planning for the campaign, however, we will make certain that the solicitation is handled by someone more to your liking.

"That darn executive director is always trying to butter me up. Lay off. She should pay attention to some of the people who don't have so much to give but are darn important to the agency for other reasons."

• That's good advice. We can make the point with her outside the written report to be submitted.

THE FLOW AND RHYTHM OF AN INTERVIEW

"Gosh, this is just like group therapy—your interview has a beginning, a middle part, and an ending." More than one interviewee has made this comment. Indeed, a good session will proceed in stages:

• A review of the request letter, questions from the interviewee ("Why me?"), and an explanation of what will take place.

• The heart of the matter: questions posed by counsel about the case, prospective leadership, and sources of support (as well as personal willingness to see others and make a personal contribution).

• A conclusion, in which responses are reviewed, confidentiality again assured, and the interviewee told what will happen next (the report, planning for a campaign, solicitation).

Maintaining control: a consultant's experience. An interview can go off track easily. In one case, a 92-year-old retired architect being interviewed for a proposed orchestra campaign refused to answer the query about those who might be effective in asking others for support. "If I tell you, then you will know which solicitor to send, and it will cost me a great deal of money," he replied. Later he recanted. "I really wasn't very nice about it. You should send Sally Smith to see me." As I learned later, the old fox had deliberately misled me. When Sally did call during an early phase of the campaign, she came away with $10,000 and not the anticipated $100,000. It turned out that Sally was a distant relative much in the gentleman's debt. Fortunately for the orchestra and unfortunately for the architect, he died six months later and left the full $100,000 to his beloved symphonic organization in his will!

In another instance, a generous prior donor to a school said at the outset of another interview that she was terribly upset about the board's firing of the organization's executive director, who had

77

become a close personal friend. She added that she was disgusted and fed up—totally disapproving of the procedures employed in the dismissal. I asked if we might terminate the interview and try again at the end of the study period. By then, of course, she had all of the facts about the dismissal and had decided that the organization was more important to her than the friendship. Her responses were now positive, and she made a substantial pledge when the campaign was launched.

A final example recalls the initial eight interviews for an organization of distinguished lawyers and judges which had been disastrous. All had insisted on re-stating counsel's questions and then providing answers which were useless. "What you really mean, young man, is . . ." At the ninth interview, with a sage attorney who had been a leading figure in the group for three decades, I decided to ask for guidance. After asking which people I had seen, he explained, "By the luck of the draw, you managed to see eight litigators in those first interviews. They make a living by behaving in that way. You will have to find a way around it." The answer hit me: If I told the story of the initial encounters and the sage lawyer's explanation, I might be able to stop the assault of question re-statements. It worked. As I met other litigators, the interviews began with the anecdote. All laughed a bit nervously but knowingly in response—and were careful to answer my questions precisely (with no new questions raised and irrelevant answers provided)!

Double-checking responses: a consultant's experience. The first ten interviews in a precampaign study for one of the country's most rigorous independent day schools had produced horrible results. All of those seen were parents, and all had said: "I really hate the school. They treat parents as if they were dirt and pay no attention to us. In fact, no one will listen to any questions or complaints." It was so bad that we cut off discussion about possible support for a capital campaign! I then went back to a group of staff members and trustees to explain my dismay. No one, at first, could think of a way to get beyond this problem. Finally, a staff member suggested that we add a second question, following a negative response, about how the parents' son or daughter felt about the school. And we set forth on the remaining interviews.

Each time a parent said, "I hate . . .," we followed up with: "And how about Johnny or Jane?" The response here was the same in all succeeding interviews: "What do you mean, my child can't wait to get up in the morning and leave for school. The kids love the place. It's the parents who are mistreated."

It took time to turn things around, but an effective parent-relations campaign was instituted with dramatic impact. Key parents were invited to dinners at the homes of the headmaster or trustees. All listened to complaints, most of which focused on the school being too demanding. Parents simply wanted to be assured that the story wasn't all negative. We had alumni present at events for parents, and could assure parents that the college-placement record of the school was proof that the flame was worth the candle. Furthermore, these successful alumni gave evidence, through their own lives and careers, that the school had done a fine job and that no one had really suffered significantly from the demanding approach.

In the campaign itself parents were the key, and their gifts brought the drive to a $5.7 million total against a goal of $5 million. And it was astounding to record responses from parents toward the drive's concluding phase, when they were approached in the tele-marketing process (see chapter 8). The average commitment was at least 50 percent higher than that recorded in similar programs for other schools that had used the procedure.

Interviews as education: a consultant's experience. Several years ago, while conducting the final interview in a study for a boarding school with a very affluent constituency, I found myself explaining to a young alumnus that everyone who had participated so far was of the mind that the school's moment to seek endowment had arrived. "You ought to have learned more about me prior to this meeting," he said, "and then you would not be surprised by what I am going to tell you. Forget about endowment, that's not important. This school should raise money to put up new buildings, paint what we have, and make certain that the grounds are in tip-top shape. That's what really counts. We've got to impress prospective students and their families. The heck with endowment."

Remembering that the young man's father, one of the country's major industrialists, had endowed faculty chairs at several universities, I was taken aback but decided to go right on with the interview for the moment. Ten minutes later, after my interviewee saw that I was just posing questions and not pushing to change his mind, he suddenly asked: "By the way, what is 'endowment?' " I couldn't believe that his father had never told him, but decided that a simple explanation was in order. After indicating that gifts for this purpose are not expended, and that only the income earned is spent to increase faculty compensation and provide scholarships, the young man scratched his chin and said that the concept was "very interesting." We then completed the session, and I put the incident out of mind. Two months later this alumnus decided to endow a chair. In fact, he endowed the director of development position! When I had an opportunity a bit later to ask him why he had come to this decision, he explained: "Once I knew what endowment was all about, it seemed to me that the school should have the best person available for this particular job so that we could improve fund-raising performance. I felt that the man now doing the job should be paid well so that we could keep him. If my gift will help, what better investment could I make?"

And so the only endowed development chair in the country, as far as anyone in the fund-raising industry knows, came into being at a very small New England school.

INTERVIEW FOLLOW-UP

Most consultants maintain private notes from each interview, remembering at the same time that the interviewees have been assured that anything written down during the session is for the interviewer's use only. The major value of a consultant's notes is to provide the material for the assessment of a proposed campaign's feasibility. But they are also helpful reminders to consultants when they write letters to interviewees, thanking them for the meetings and reviewing, in a general way, the ground covered. That follow-up letter will lead several of those interviewed to write back with additional information, usually mentioning more key prospects. If the consultants send blind carbons of their letters to one key staff person or volunteer leader, it will also help the organization to keep track of progress. Nothing specific from the conversation is ever included, so the promised confidentiality is maintained.

INTERPRETING THE INFORMATION

Different consultants have different techniques for tabulating responses. Some use a scoring method to track how the interviewees have responded to proposed objectives. ("One third like the plans for a new library; two thirds want no part of the proposed site".) Another approach, after one is assured that plans and projects meet with general approval, is to focus on questions of leadership and donor potential. This approach develops statistics on the number of times individuals are cited by others for solicitation ability and how often potential donors of major gifts are mentioned in the givers' categories. Counsel must cross-check to make certain that some overwhelming solicitation favorites have not insisted, personally, that they "won't do it again for this or any other cause." Similarly, an organization cannot count on a $1 million pledge from a corporation just because most of the interviewees insist that this is what should happen. What really matters is how those representing the company respond during the interviews. Other responses to watch with care:

- If board members who have collectively endorsed the proposed campaign's objectives privately indicate that several other charitable institutions rate ahead of this one, there is little chance that they will make significant contributions as solicitors or donors.

- No matter how many interviewees feel that "Joe is a top prospect," the assembled statistics will mean little in this area if Joe's attorney and trust officer have indicated that a contribution simply will not be possible, even if Joe himself insists that he will make a major commitment.

- If people who have been named many times as potential leaders feel reluctant to ask for support, they can be told later by counsel that their peers see it differently. That knowledge always instills confidence and turns reluctant individuals into cautious enthusiasts.

ADJUSTING STUDY METHODOLOGY FOR TRENDS

After counsel has completed half of the interviews in a study and clearcut trends have developed, it is possible to use the data already gathered to give the succeeding interviews a slightly different thrust. The following story shows how. The chairman of one college board (our client) was hard-pressed for time, and our only chance for an interview before a report on the study was due came during a three-hour trip by limousine from his home to the college's campus. Wondering what I would talk about for that length of time (most interviews last 30-45 minutes), I decided to set the stage for the campaign by sharing most of my findings to date with him.

Before I could open the discussion, this chief executive officer of one of the country's largest financial-services companies decided to tell me that there was a limit to what corporations would contribute and that most would not give at all in this campaign until they were certain that individual graduates had already contributed generously. I decided to change directions and said, "Why don't we start at the beginning and let me interview you as if you were just another alumnus?" He agreed to this procedure, and we quickly moved through the qustions until we reached the one about potential donors of $1 million or more. Being forthright at every point, he responded that his company and several others *could* give at that level but would not do so until individual donors had done their part.

At this stage, it seemed worth the gamble to switch plans again, so I went back and briefed my interviewee on results to date: Most of the top donors of the previous drive were still paying off 10-year pledges (such long pledges being a major strategic error in the earlier campaign), and felt that the companies had never carried a fair share of the burden in supporting the college, and said that they would not give one more penny toward a building project that still carried a large debt burden (their blaming this situation on the trustees, who headed large companies and had voted for the project which led to the debt obligation).

Fortunately, it was possible to quote statistics backing up these assertions. The board chairman began to think about the implications of this informal report, and I could tell he was considering what difference it would make if his and other major corporations gave at the million-dollar level. There was no point in pushing further; the seed had been planted.

Several weeks later, the board chairman told his fellow trustees (after our study report had been presented): "You've heard the story, we have no choice. Several of us must give at the million-dollar level and contribute first in the campaign toward that debt. If we do, I am convinced that individuals will then give generously (as their previous pledges are completed) toward other aspects of our program." Before the meeting ended, each trustee in a position to do so had made a pledge for his company in proportion to the lead gift announced by the chairman.

Counsel had "sold" by not selling. Remaining a bit aloof and objective—just presenting the facts—had won the day.

REPORTING RESULTS DURING THE STUDY

Completion of the study raises several issues, some of which are quite sensitive. Because interviewees were promised that their responses would be private, you and the consultant will have to protect the confidentiality of some parts of the study. The board will have to receive and approve the report. Results must be shared with the persons who were interviewed. And, if the study's results are negative, the board will face some hard decisions.

Progress Reports

Few heads of gift-supported institutions can resist the temptation to ask the consultants how the interviews are going, so eager are they to know how they are perceived by constituents. It helps when the consultant can say, "You're doing just fine. The quality of your leadership is recognized by those we have seen." If you are in such a position, keep in mind that the consultant is not asking questions about you personally. If a spate of negative comments about staff or volunteers accumulates, they must be dealt with by counsel. It takes experience to know the difference between substantive complaints and minor gripes—the key issue is the nature of the problem and the people talking about it. If the matters are serious, counsel can encourage an individual to take the issue back to the person in the organization who is in a position to answer the question. A persistent problem (from "the headmaster does not greet the buses in the morning" to failure of an executive director to produce financial reports in advance of board meetings) can be dealt with by having counsel discuss the items with the staff member or volunteer quietly—never attributing the matter to any specific individuals.

Consultants always prefer to complete the full set of interviews in a study before rendering assessments; nervous boards, on the other hand, want preliminary reports. Somehow, a balance must be struck. It is useful to meet with the ad hoc committee mid-way through the study to present an oral report on progress to date. Although it is difficult to avoid being specific, and everyone wants to know the numbers ("how much can we raise?"), broad answers usually satisfy most of those concerned. Typically, counsel might say: "We are testing $10 million; right now it appears that somewhere between $5.5 million and $7.5 million is feasible; it could be less or more, depending on how things work out in the final third of interviews, in which half of the best prospects will be seen." If word spreads about "what the consultants are going to recommend," those still to be interviewed will wonder why anyone is bothering to continue with the study, and will feel that their participation will be a waste of time.

Confidentiality

The confidentiality of the precampaign study will continue to be an issue throughout the campaign. Much of the study's information can be shared with staff members and key volunteers as long as remarks are not attributed to those who made them and sources are never revealed. Counsel can share comments about how much the major prospects should be asked for, conclusions as to who should do the soliciting of specific prospects, and how the entire campaign should be presented and characterized.

By the time you reach later phases of the campaign, you will have information from other sources to take into account. Regional meetings may have been held, during which friends of an organization commented on the giving potential of prospects living in their area. An organization's research office might have fresh clues about a prospect's recent business success (not revealed during consultant's interview). A close friend or business associate of a prospect might suggest a different and more effective approach. Counsel's role is to exercise discretion and control over all confidential information while assuring, at the same time, that all people involved in the campaign have the data they need.

When the Results Are Negative

If the proposed new headquarters for an organization will cost $3 million but the precampaign study indicates that only $1 million will be available, a board knows where it stands. The structure cannot be built with voluntary support alone. Of course, this does not mean that any fund-raising campaign is doomed. The consultant is simply telling the board what is feasible at the present. But studies should not be initiated on a black-or-white, yes-no basis alone. An organization should not say: "We want to know if $3 million can be raised, and if the answer is 'no' or 'not at this time' we will abandon all fund-raising plans." An inexperienced consultant might take such guidance literally and believe that the organization wants a "yes" or "no" answer (nothing more, nothing less).

The issue is usually more complicated. Funds are required for a variety of needs, and partial funding can be of significant help. The balance can be borrowed, added to a school's tuition, or, for a health agency, even covered by third-party reimbursement. Money is fungible, and if funds can be raised for scholarships at a college but not for construction (unfortunately, it is usually the other way around), the institution's operating requirements might be met in the financial aid category, thus releasing dollars previously held for that purpose to cover the planned renovations.

The consultant's real assignment is to help organizations obtain needed funds, not just to try to "prove" what is or is not possible. It is essential to take the position that solutions must be found—even if they are far different from those foreseen by the selection panel that chose the firm. Consultants often come back to an organization in a report (or earlier) to make suggestions such as:

- "Your best friends are not responding well to your plans but have great respect for the institution and want to help. Why don't we come to terms with them and lower the goal, adjust objectives, or recognize that the full job cannot be done with philanthropic support alone?" A board member is bound to insist on going right ahead with the campaign for those funds and on continuing until the money is in hand, even if it takes an extra year or two. More than likely, counsel already knows that this particular program (with its specific objectives) will not succeed in two or even 20 extra years. Unfortunately, dragging out a projected time-frame rarely solves the underlying problems. Usually, more are created: Annual giving suffers, the organization is perceived as always raising money, or more pressing needs cannot be met because the current campaign is still before the public.

- "The annual giving base is too narrow; let's work on that before we try to raise substantial capital."

- "Faculty salaries are just not of interest. Scholarship aid is. Let's work on that side, and you will have money released in your operating budget to increase salaries."

- "The goal is simply unobtainable, but your organization's friends are willing to pay more for subscriptions. A more modest goal and increased box office results will add up to the overall financial objective you had in mind initially."

- "A major segment of the constituency is not philanthropically inclined. The study reveals that they would rather pay more tuition than increase their annual support, despite the tax advantages. So you should consider higher rates and then focus your fund-raising program on a smaller audience, and do it in a quiet way."

- "The Board is unwilling to carry its share of the assignment in both giving and asking. Its members must be convinced that the case is compelling and urgent. And it may well be that some trustees should be replaced or the board expanded to include more individuals who are in a position to be helpful." This is not to say, however, that all trustees are asked to serve for their fund-raising capability alone. What a boring situation that would be—and hardly helpful to an institution needing many types of skills and experience in its board members.

THE INTERNAL AUDIT—REPORTING RESULTS

At the same time the feasibility study is conducted, the consultant evaluates your organization's resources. This evaluation is generally referred to as the internal audit. The internal audit section of the consultant's report usually focuses on additional resources required. If more staff, renovated offices, and new equipment are needed, there is no better time to obtain board approval for the expenditures, particularly since the costs will be met through campaign proceeds.

A study report must provide an assessment of the development staff's ability to provide the back-up support needed by campaign volunteers. To avoid dwelling on staff problems in a written document, a consultant can work behind the scenes to review and resolve personnel problems before the report is prepared. Situations will include:

- When, for example, the development director learns from the consultant, during a private interview, that the task at hand is really beyond his or her capacity. Changes in assignment or a move to another institution can be initiated in discussions with the person involved, the salaried head of the organization, and board leadership.

- The staff development officer and the consultant assess the function and determine that more help from the firm will be needed in a campaign than the board realized at the outset of the study.

- All agree that a total reorganization of the function is required, and the adjustments are made before the study report is issued.

USING THE FINAL REPORT

Seeking Board Acceptance

A board should not be asked to "approve" the document submitted by counsel at the end of a study; the correct term is "accept." The findings, conclusions, and recommendations should stand. After all, the material is no more than a reflection of the organization's own constituents as viewed by the consultant. Through various resolutions, taken up apart from the report, a board can authorize several campaign steps to be taken such as setting the goal and appointing a steering committee.

It is often helpful to have one or two board members review a draft of the study report before it is carried to the entire board. Misunderstandings and mistakes can be cleared up, and enthusiasm for the campaign rekindled—remember, three months will have elapsed since the study was authorized. In coming to grips with the report's conclusions and recommendations, board members will compromise with each other. An adept chairperson might say, "If we can only raise enough money to do this project now, we'll get to your favorite project in the next stage of the continuing development effort"—and thus arrive at a consensus about the scope of the campaign to be initiated. If, instead, the campaign is authorized by something like a 10-4 vote, an organization will rarely achieve its goals. A capital fund-raising effort requires the full support and backing of those who govern an institution. No drive should begin until consensus has been achieved on the drive's objectives, dollar goal, leadership, and organizational pattern.

Use the right tool for the right job: a consultant's experience. Some years ago, a consultant submitted a report to the board of a child-care agency and was told that the executive committee would consider it and tell the consultant how to "fix it up." Counsel was not to be present for the discussion. It turned out that a faction of the board had hoped to use the document to fire the development director, a person who had won high marks during the study from most of the interviewees. When the firm learned that the meeting was for head-hunting, not fund-raising, purposes, it refused to abide by the suggested procedure and offered to withdraw immediately from the assignment unless invited to take part in the executive committee's discussion of the report. Counsel was asked to participate. The report had focused on fund raising, not personnel matters, and disappointed the board faction (heavily represented on the committee) that wanted the staff member's resignation. Much later, counsel was informed that the report had been inadequate and that the firm's services would no longer be required. So much for a bad situation. The moral: Use fund-raising consultants to help your organization meet fund-raising objectives, not to solve personnel problems.

Sharing Results with Interviewees

Before the study begins, counsel should ask the board for permission to tell interviewees that the project's results will be shared with everyone who participated. Ideally, the full document presented to the board should be sent to those who were interviewed— along with a letter of appreciation from the chairperson thanking the individual for taking part. If the report, as actually submitted later, is just too lengthy for use in this way, an abridged version can be mailed. But it is important that the flavor of the basic document be retained to reflect the actual responses received, even if it is critical of an institution's performance and plans. Showing how your organization is perceived, warts and all, indicates that the organization is prepared to make adjustments in its program. There is no better way to prepare the interviewees (your best prospects) for solicitation than to take them into your confidence. Demonstrating to them that they have been heard is a step in the right direction. Comments of the interviewees will have been set forth, although the remarks are not attributed to them. Circulation of the document shows that the organization is willing to bring problems into the open for consideration by a larger group than the board alone. This approach builds long-term support.

A Second Study?

It does not happen often, but you might have to conduct another study for one or more of the following reasons:

- The board concludes that the first study was inadequate.

- Strategy has changed, to pursue new objectives or to adjust to a different economic environment.

- Well into the campaign, a decision is made to change consultants.

A new firm will want to do a study in its own way. You will feel reluctant to start again and bother your constituents with yet another series of interviews, but that is precisely what is required. The need for a second study can be explained to them in several ways:

- "We were not satisfied with the initial study, and quite frankly feel that it is essential to check our results because the program under discussion is so important."

- "... for those reasons, we feel that it is imperative to change our goals and are asking a small number of the organization's best friends to meet with a consultant who has just a few more questions to ask."

- "When we conducted the original study, the organization was not yet fully committed to going forward with the program you reviewed. We have made adjustments suggested by you and others, and are convinced that we are on the right track. We would appreciate having your comments on the revised program through the consultants we have now retained to help us."

When a campaign has stalled, a second study is crucial because the organization gains time to regroup, and the consultant who is just coming up to speed has a chance to determine why things went wrong. Meanwhile, sophisticated donors will recognize that a human error has been made and that the organization is smart enough to make a fresh start instead of continuing down the wrong road. Finally, a board embarked on a drive with limited enthusiasm can renew its commitment to the objectives if a second study confirms or adjusts original impressions of donor and leadership potential.

A reputable firm will pick up a campaign in the middle and offer guidance only if it can meet, on a confidential basis, with those who will determine whether a drive succeeds. Unless a second study is undertaken, previous errors or problems will be compounded, no matter how wise the outside advisor might be. Nothing is worse than having guidance from a consultant who can speak from general experience gained elsewhere but who has no specific knowledge of this campaign.

Chapter 10

PREPARING FOR THE CAMPAIGN TO GO PUBLIC

Good things come to those who wait.
—a maxim

Human nature being what it is, most board members can hardly wait to share the good news of a positive precampaign study with friends and supporters. "We're going to have a campaign and everyone should know about it," they want to proclaim. "The study proves it can be done, and we're ready to go." However, the organization is not ready to go anywhere, let alone make its intentions public. A successful fund-raising program will proceed quietly at this point to develop a comprehensive plan and to establish the campaign's nucleus fund. The public announcement of the campaign should occur after these steps, demonstrating to a broader constituency more than initial success and that the campaign is under good leadership. "After all," you will be able to say, "our close friends have already backed the campaign."

However, it is important to know what you are planning for. Therefore, this chapter outlines the first phases of the campaign and its general activity and timetable guidelines. The next three chapters then address actual planning, training, and interaction between your organization and the consultant.

THE NUCLEUS FUND

Your capital campaign cannot succeed unless the governing group sets an example for all others who will be asked for support.

Major prospective contributors beyond the board will ask, "What has your board done individually and collectively?" The trustees' giving record must demonstrate a commitment to your cause and show that their gifts are at least as substantial as what is being asked of people beyond the governance group. These initial, sizable contributions from trustees constitute the all-important *nucleus fund*.

A capital campaign's nucleus fund encompasses the gifts of trustees past and present, as well as those of their families. On occasion, the fund can be expanded to include gifts from trustees elected during the campaign and commitments from up to 10 more close friends of the institution. But you should be sure never to borrow too much from other designated groups of donors just to put more gifts into the nucleus fund.

Setting a goal or target figure for the nucleus fund is essential. Most groups retaining counsel for a precampaign study want the answer even before the vital interviews have been undertaken: "What will you expect from us board members—15 percent, 25 percent, or 50 percent of the total campaign?" Obviously, this question must not be dealt with until the consultant has figured out both the board's immediate potential for giving and how that meshes with the potential of the balance of the organization's constituency.

There are no rules of thumb in this area, but experience has shown that successful drives often follow these patterns:

- A social service agency with a large board (35 members) and few major donor prospects in its non-board constituency, might require 60 percent of its goal to come from the governing body in a $3 million drive.

- A major university with a small board of 15 members and a large alumni group of 35,000 might need only 15 percent of a $50 million goal from its trustees.

- A hospital with a board of 30 and a constituency being asked to contribute to a capital drive for the first time will probably need 25 percent of a $5 million campaign from the governing body.

- A boarding school with a wealthy alumni and parent constituency might need 30 percent of its $6 million goal contributed by the trustees.

Typically, half of the six-figure and seven-figure pledges in a campaign are made by the board during the initial nucleus fund stage of a campaign. But counsel's task is to convince the trustees that the money cannot be raised "on average." The nucleus fund solicitations—trustees calling on trustees—are a microcosm of the full campaign to follow. There will be a spread of commitments from token and modest to substantial and pace-setting. When a goal of $2 million is established for a nucleus fund and there are 20 board members and 17 former trustees, someone is bound to say, "That's just $100,000 a trustee even if the past board members do nothing." For some donors, that "average" will be far too low (and will get them off the hook rather inexpensively); for others, the amount will be mind-boggling. The solution is to have counsel create a special level-of-giving table for this phase of the project (see table 10-1).

TABLE 10-1: Nucleus fund level-of-giving table

Range	Number Needed	Total
$ 500,000	1	$ 500,000
250,000	2	500,000
150,000	2	300,000
100,000	2	200,000
50,000	4	200,000
25,000	6	150,000
10,000	10	100,000
5,000 and under	10	50,000

It is crucial that these commitments be sought quietly and privately—and under the guidance of an experienced consultant. If the projections are realized in a period of three to four months, it is difficult indeed to fail in the more public aspects of the drive to follow. And if the total is far under what has been anticipated, no real harm has been done. The overall campaign objective can be scaled back accordingly, and no one beyond the Board will ever know the difference.

If the target figure is missed, counsel might well still suggest "going for the full goal." Ordinarily, this judgment is based on insights about giving habits picked up during the confidential interviews. Perhaps one major donor will be the type of individual who prefers to give both the initial $250,000 and the final $250,000 to a campaign. So it is possible for the consultant to project that, ultimately, the full goal for the nucleus fund will be realized and thus not much risk is being taken just because the total seems short of the mark at the moment.

THE CAMPAIGN PLAN

Most institutions can hardly wait to see a full-blown plan that describes how each stage of the campaign will unfold. A useful timetable plan for a capital campaign, developed by you, your staff, and the consultant, should include these elements:

- Counsel's report on the precampaign study

- 12-month (or longer) timetable

- Table of organization chart (who reports to whom)

- Chart on who is responsible for what at each stage

- Case statement

- Position descriptions for key volunteer leaders (based on the "who does what" chart)

- Fact sheet on the organization

- Essential financial data on the organization (budget or audit statement)

The assembled material becomes the "bible" for the campaign. A loose-leaf notebook format is recommended so that new material (brochure, newsletters) can be added and existing documents can be changed.

The best approach to the matter is for counsel to set forth an outline of the timetable (see table 10-2).

TABLE 10-2: Sample capital campaign timetable

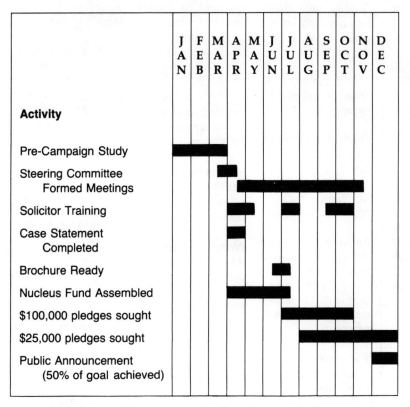

Knowing who will be responsible for what is almost as important to volunteers as understanding the sequence of activities being pursued, especially if this is your organization's first campaign. It is advisable, therefore, to develop another chart that describes duties and responsibilities in the campaign's early months (see Table 10-3).

A typical campaign proceeds through the following steps in its first three months, with distinct roles for all of the participants.

In the campaign's early months, many things begin to happen at once: Roles and responsibilities begin to overlap. A chart like that shown in table 10-3 helps the organization and the consultant keep a finger on the campaign to make certain that:

TABLE 10-3: Sample capital campaign timetable for first three months

	Consultant	Staff	Steering Committee
M O N T H 1	Guides each meeting, planning for the session and guiding the leadership. Trains committee in effective solicitation techniques. Trains staff and helps develop internal systems. Completes work on draft case statement.	Prepares all papers needed for the campaign meetings—assignment sheets, background on prospects. Develops draft material on campaign policy matters. Refines the case that had been prepared as a first draft by counsel.	Approves the timetable and budget. Carries out the first solicitations—on each other. Approves major campaign policies. Adds to initial membership.
M O N T H 2	Prepares material on "how to solicit" and "how to give." Suggests target figures for initial prospects. Recommends proper solicitor for each call to be made.	Works with counsel on implementing previous report recommendations on staffing, systems, and procedures. Prospect research stepped up. Close liaison maintained with counsel in regard to meeting agendas and follow-up materials needed.	Addresses the question of permanent leadership for the committee. Meets every three weeks. Keeps board members informed. Solicitation circle widens to include full board and other close friends. Reviews the case statement.
M O N T H 3	Develops a campaign plan, expanding upon study report recommendations. Assists individual members of the committee in preparing for calls. Reviews all recommendations in report to monitor progress.	Initiates publication planning (designers interviewed). Briefs other on the organization's staff about campaign plans.	

- the staff is not becoming overloaded;

- the volunteers are not biting off more than they can digest at one sitting—taking three or four solicitation assignments at a time (not ten or twelve);

- timetables are being maintained;

- items needed later are started (planning for the brochure must be initiated even though it won't be printed for months); and

- a budget procedure is established;

- confidence of the solicitors continues to build.

While developing a campaign plan, a tug-of-war might occur between you and counsel. Your inclination will be toward having a comprehensive plan, but the consultant might prefer to schedule one step at a time so that the focus remains on the task at hand and not on what might happen in a month. Counsel might want to maintain a flexible approach to ensure that successive steps are initiated only after the projected level of support is reached. In other words, actual progress in raising dollars—not time—dictates the schedule. From this point of view, an institution should not move from the solicitation of $100,000 commitments to $10,000 pledges just because a schedule says that the time has arrived. The governing question is: "Have we raised enough $100,000 pledges to move on now?"

Consultants and firms who engage in short-term (three- to five-month) drives for community agencies such as Y's, libraries, and churches, would argue that a day-by-day timetable forces staff and leadership to maintain a schedule by pressing supporters to "give now or we'll fall behind and begin to fail." A different attitude must prevail in a large, multimillion dollar program that might take several years to complete. The ultimate success of such a campaign depends on the early commitment of six-figure and seven-figure pledges. It might take weeks and months for donor decisions at this level, and the drive cannot proceed until the pledges are in hand because failure to secure them will lead to the lowering of sights in succeeding stages of the program.

THE PUBLIC ANNOUNCEMENT

The culmination of the campaign's first phase is, finally, the public announcement. Inexperienced volunteers are eager to know when the campaign will "go public." They are convinced that things will begin to happen just as soon "as we tell the world that we are in a campaign." For them, the most important line on the timetable is "Public Announcement—June 15th." It seems reasonable to expect that an eager public will respond rapidly to the announcement (that funds will begin to arrive over the transom). If, under the guidance of counsel, you have proceeded in the proven step-by-step way, the announcement will come when you have reached 35-50 percent of your goal and will have a campaign plan in place. This significant progress on funds already contributed makes the public announcement credible—the audience receiving it knows immediately that the campaign being announced has a good chance of succeeding. Nothing assures success more than clear evidence that "the job can be done."

Chapter 11

GETTING ORGANIZED

We have met the enemy and he is us.
—Walt Kelly

A fund-raising campaign depends on the effective cooperation of two groups: a steering committee of the volunteer leaders and your own institutional staff. Even if the precampaign study predicts success, a campaign will achieve its goals only if the best participants are recruited, if they are trained properly, and if they are brought into the campaign with the guidance of counsel. Recruitment and training is one of the important tasks of the campaign's first phase.

FORMING THE STEERING COMMITTEE

Your first organizational step is to appoint a campaign steering committee. If a campaign chairperson has not been enlisted by this point, the committee can be named by the board chairperson, who will serve as chairperson pro tem. In fact, it is often wise not to have a chairperson in place until the nucleus fund has been completed and there is solid evidence that the drive can reach its potential. Only four or five members should be appointed at the outset. They, in turn, select additional candidates. The steering committee is responsible for several tasks: soliciting contributions from each other and then the full board; communicating regularly with the board about the campaign's progress and problems; developing working relationships between staff and counsel; and assuring that people and funds are made available as needed. When selecting its additional members, the core group should seek others who are effective in fund raising, representative of the organization as a whole, and held in high regard by the constituency at large.

A steering committee for the future: a consultant's experience. When selecting the steering committee, remember that your current campaign is also preparation for your next campaign. At a well-known boarding school, our firm once recommended that women graduates be added to the campaign steering committee right from the start. The school had become coeducational a decade earlier. A year later, when the group decided to increase its size, counsel pointed out that no action had yet been taken on our recommendation. In twenty years, we suggested, nearly half of the active graduates would be women if present enrollment trends were to continue. Two fine female graduates were nominated for membership on the spot. The steering committee then reflected a larger constituency and was prepared to initiate those who would be leading the school's fund-raising programs for several decades. Keeping this long view is important, in fact, not just in selecting your committee but in all facets of the campaign.

For more on working with the steering committee, see chapter 13.

VOLUNTEER LEADERSHIP

Conventional wisdom dictates that any institution prevail upon a "name" candidate for leadership of its major fund-raising effort; a common alternative is "someone who is retired and now has lots of time." Neither course is recommended. A "name" is just that—as time goes by, that person's lack of presence will demoralize everyone. And the retired person is no longer in the mainstream and is often concerned with new interests.

The appropriate selection is a busy individual who cares deeply about the organization. You need to be certain that the person believes in the case and is convinced of its urgency and that the potential leader will expect you to spell out the precise nature and timing of the task. It will not be sufficient to tell a prospective leader that "we just need your name on the letterhead and your time for a few key calls." Having met most of the leadership possibilities during the study, counsel can give important advice about the best candidate. It is often a good idea to have the consultant give the leading candidate a private briefing on the study, a perspective on dollar potential, and a view of who will or should take major roles in the drive. During this discussion, counsel can develop a clear job description with the leader, so all parties will know precisely what is expected of the chairperson and others involved.

What if you have to "fire" a campaign leader in the middle of a campaign? This potential, and not unusual, problem should be under consideration right from the outset, so hasty solutions are not necessary. One solution is to appoint a co-chair, another is to name a "completion phase" leader. Or you can divide the campaign into several segments—nucleus fund, major gifts, and everything else— each a year's duration. If different leaders can be appointed for each phase, the disruption of losing one leader will not be so great.

BUILDING THE STAFF—HOW TO DO IT AND WHAT TO LOOK FOR

Campaigns for large institutions tend to be "staff-driven." Staff members who are veterans of previous engagements know what is expected of them and will make good use of counsel as a sounding board or to reinforce key strategy policies with board members. Small institutions tend to be "counsel-driven," and the consultant will play a larger role in, first, building and training staff and then in guiding their work.

If you determine that additional staff is required—whether a part-time secretary for a small agency or several people at various levels of experience and talent for, say, a large university—there is a systematic way to proceed. Job descriptions should be prepared and agreed to by staff leadership, volunteers, and the consultant. Institutional personnel policies should be followed—with one exception—by observing commitments to promote from within; posting job descriptions internally, and by honoring equal opportunity and affirmative action commitments. The single exception is salary. A person employed by contract for a set period will command higher amounts than would be paid to permanent staff. This fact must be recognized by all involved with the program.

A rush to "staff up" quickly can lead to many errors—resumes are taken at face value, only listed references are checked, and personal habits are not investigated. But you are not looking for full disclosure of finances and lifestyle, only an inquiry about characteristics that could be a problem when a temporary staff member begins to represent the organization to its public. Traits to watch for include:

- abuse of alcohol or drugs (the biggest problem of all);

- an inability to be punctual (particularly for committee meetings);

- lack of respect for deadlines;

- a deep-seated feeling of resentment toward people of affluence;

- excessive aggressiveness;

- lack of tact; and

- an inability to separate professional relationships and friendships.

An executive search firm can save you time and money in finding your high-level staff needs. Reference checks are much easier when conducted by a third party. Of course, the fund-raising consulting firm might help, but they should retain a focus on fund raising. Protracted searches could waste their valuable time.

TRAINING SOLICITORS

Solicitors are the volunteers who go out to donors and ask for contributions. It is likely that your organization has many people who could be effective solicitors but are reluctant to become involved because they do not understand the case or they do not know how to make fund-raising calls. It is probably true that they do not, in fact, know how to approach a donor. (And you should beware of those who easily say, "Of course I can do it; fund raising is the same as selling any product.") But an experienced consultant can train an organization's volunteers to be effective solicitors. Your consultant will have worked with similar volunteers in other drives, and will know what will make the volunteers confident enough in their own ability to move forward. Having conducted the pre-campaign study, the consultant will also know which solicitors will be most effective with which prospects, at which level to seek support from which prospect—toward which component of the institution's objectives, which messages about the institution should be conveyed, and how basic solicitation techniques should be adjusted and then applied for this particular organization with this case and at this time.

It is the consultant's task to bring the organization's case and solicitation techniques together for the volunteers. While the solicitors can be told what to do and how to do it, a better method is the use of playlets that committee members act out to learn what works and what does not. To begin a playlet, counsel presents a hypothetical situation and asks for volunteers to act out the parts. One of those situations might go like this: Joe Smith is a former board member who gives $1,000 annually and contributed $25,000 in our last campaign. Since that time, he has remained active in the school's affairs. We know that his company, XYZ Widgets, has had two banner years in a row, and Joe owns 70 percent of the stock. Joe is known for his interest in scholarship students. Sam Jones, a board member who is chairman of the campaign steering committee, will make this call. Sam gives $1,000 a year to the annual fund and has pledged $100,000 to the campaign—having given $25,000 a decade ago to the previous major drive. Sam knows Joe well in business circles, but they are not close socially. They share an interest in the school, and have had overlapping terms on the board. Both are alumni, and Joe's son is a current student at the school. Sam's task is to ask for a $150,000 commitment from Joe in addition to his continuing annual support. Before the play begins, counsel spells out the aims:

1. Explain at the outset why you have come to visit.

2. Build the case for scholarships and make certain that he is interested.

3. When asking for the pledge, divide the amount by three ("Will you consider giving $50,000 a year for the next three years to endow a scholarship?").

4. Determine when his decision will be made and given to you.

5. Conclude your conversation in twenty minutes.

To make this presentation effective for both the participants and the audience, counsel must take a firm hand in guiding the proceedings. If a point has been missed or a wrong approach has been introduced, the consultant should step in. When appropriate, the "actors" should be praised for good lines and criticized when they digress.

The important point is that the playlet will quickly lead the committee members to feel that they can learn solicitation techniques. The exercise may also lead to revision of the case statement. In acting out the playlets, questions will arise which were not dealt with in early drafts of the document.

Training sessions become more complex as work on the nucleus fund continues and counsel introduces more elaborate playlets in which a team of two solicitors might call on a husband and wife (she has the money, but tends to withdraw from the discussion when her husband is excluded from a conversation). Because some of the first calls will have occurred, the group can dramatize those calls as they actually took place. The volunteers can also work on situations in which a gift now is just not possible and the prospects must be addressed in terms of planned gifts (bequests and annuity trusts).

Later in a campaign, when more committees are formed to reach a larger constituency, staff members can lead these training sessions themselves. But when a drive is barely under way, the outside consultant can be more effective in chiding a recalcitrant volunteer or making light of a flub. As you might imagine, egos can be ruffled. Example: We had a chilling experience some years ago at a college for women. Halfway through a training session for the full board, a young woman stood up and said, "That's enough of this silly business. We know what to do." A man who was down the table from her stood up quickly (he was chairman of an $8 billion company) and responded, before I could say a word, "It might be silly for you, but I need this training and believe that the rest of you should pay attention if we are to raise the money needed. Let's get on with it." We did.

Counsel's role continues as the initial calls begin. Even though committee members have been trained, virtually no one will feel comfortable with the assignments. Counsel can work individually with the committee members to make certain that each knows the special interests and concerns of key prospects. Requesting consideration of an appropriate amount is also essential, and counsel can assure the solicitors that they will be close to the mark with the figures they have. Counsel should also debrief the solicitors after their first calls, to make certain that both the techniques and case are working as planned.

Chapter 12

SYSTEMS AND PROCEDURES: WORKING WITH STAFF

The first thing we should do is change all of your systems and procedures to conform with how our firm feels records should be maintained.
—A consultant more concerned with the firm's convenience then the client's real needs

When looking at your organization's fund-raising procedures, an outside consultant can make a useful contribution or suggest change merely for the sake of change and throw the organization into a tailspin. The guiding motto should be, "If it ain't broke, don't try to fix it." You should resist the consultant's plan to introduce new procedures just because the firm has used them elsewhere. Negotiation and compromise between you and the consultant are required. Some precepts are instructive for both you and the consultant when looking at your campaign organization:

- If the donor universe is substantial (more than 10,000), a specialist might well be needed for advice on data processing.

- In a campaign for $3 million, you may well be concerned with no more than 25 prospects for 90 percent of the money ultimately contributed; the institution does not need a very fancy system to keep track of two dozen individuals.

- If a data system cannot be tailored to specific needs for reaching the top prospects, look to other procedures (3 × 5 cards, file folders, or simple word processing).

- A campaign can improve discipline in an organization by insisting on acknowledging all gifts and pledges within 24 hours; by depositing checks immediately (to avoid the "Obviously, they don't really need my money." complaint); by assuring that an institution's executives and key volunteers thank donors for their commitments within a few days of the contribution's receipt.

- What works at one institution might be entirely inappropriate at another of the same size.

RUNNING THE CAMPAIGN—YOU AND THE CONSULTANT

Right from the outset, an institution's development officer and the consultant must reinforce each other. When they agree on who should be doing what, the campaign will flourish; if they cannot agree, it will suffer. Between the outside firm and the organization, theirs is the most important working relationship.

During the precampaign study, it is usually the development director's task to arrange interview appointments and make certain that the trustees and others to be seen by counsel understand the importance of the process. The consultant will be explaining to those interviewed that the development officer (not the consultant) will be providing needed services for the volunteers in the campaign that will probably follow.

As the institution's advisor, counsel should be responsible for: 1) training the development officer (both for current activities and for that day when counsel will no longer be retained); 2) serving as a sounding board for the staff person; 3) reinforcing messages which the staff members are sending to their superiors and/or key volunteers; and 4) providing an extra pair of hands when there is too much to be done at once and a few pieces need writing quickly.

The partnership works best when it is open and frank. Both the staff officer and counsel must confer on all matters for which they are responsible. If, for instance, a volunteer calls counsel directly for advice on how to approach a prospect, then counsel must inform the development officer of what took place. Similarly, if a volunteer complains to the staff member that counsel is not helping in a special area of concern, it is the development officer's job to explain the situation to the consultant so that both can get back to the volunteer and iron out the problem.

It is important that an organization's head (president, headmaster, or executive director) have open and direct access to counsel without the development officer feeling that "they have gone over my head." Consultants have been engaged to provide services for the institution as a whole. Their advice to top leaders just enhances the development officer's role—as long as everyone understands the arrangements and the counsel-development officer relationship remains mutually supportive.

Staff Meetings

As you can see, clear and unimpeded communication is an indispensable factor in a successful campaign. So that expectations are clear and the flow of information is open, you must meet regularly with counsel. Nothing is more counter-productive than meetings with counsel that are conducted without agendas. It is the consultant's responsibility to maintain a running list of major questions to review with staff and committee members in regular meetings. Well-trained development officers will maintain their own agendas. When both sets of papers are reviewed at the outset of a meeting, the important questions will be answered and priorities established on a timely basis. Your consultant is not doing a good job by arriving on the scene at the development director's office and saying, "Well, what have you done about X, Y, and Z since our last visit?" The consultant has no feeling at all for life at a gift-supported organization if that stance is used. The agenda for a meeting with your consultant might sound like this:

1. Please bring me up-to-date on progress in the key solicitations.

2. Have you had a chance to call John and ask him to approach Joe about serving on the committee?

3. Will the designer really have his sketches this week? Why don't we call him now to see how things stand?

4. Would it be helpful if I joined you later today for the meeting with the executive director on the solicitations to be completed by next week?

5. Are we having any trouble in prospect research? Should I meet with the head of that office to review our priorities again?

6. Let's prepare the agenda now for next month's meeting of the committee.

With that start, the consultant can move rapidly into other matters—a review of the budget, a check to make certain that solicitation deadlines are being met, and a discussion with the full staff on progress to date and what will be expected of each staff member during the next three months.

NOTE: You should try to avoid falling into a rut in your relationship with counsel: "We're paying for five days a month and want you here for those full days." That definition of a "day" is not very useful (for more on a consultant's day, see chapter 14). More value is often received for your investment if the consultant suggests:

- "Let's meet for two hours on Wednesday to go over our respective agendas; if we can't cover them in that amount of time, we're not on the same wave-length."

- "The next evening we should really sit down for an hour with the chairman of the campaign."

- "I would like to spend more time on the weekend re-writing our 'helpful hints' for solicitors."

- "On Monday, of course, I will be with you for that full meeting of the Board to present our progress report."

RECEIVING GIFTS—NOT THE ROLE OF THE BUSINESS OFFICER

One of the important procedures in your campaign will be how you receive gifts, and it is likely to cause you and your consultant to bump against another important person in the organization—the business officer. It is extremely difficult to run a major fund-raising program unless the office responsible for the drive receives all gifts directly and is the *only* department responsible for dealing with donors and their representatives. Counsel, and you, must enforce this rule at the highest levels within an organization for several reasons:

- If a business officer opens all the mail, delays will ensue; donors must be thanked properly and promptly.

- If an office other than development handles discussions with stockbrokers, the development office will not even be aware that a gift is being made. It becomes impossible to thank both the donor and the solicitor on a timely basis.

- If envelopes are discarded before an experienced development officer sees them, much vital information—from clues about the real source of the support, no matter what the check says, to the much-needed postmark on an envelope containing securities—may be lost.

If a business officer works directly with donors for any reason, a variety of problems will develop. There is no way for this individual to have any real understanding of the benefactors' backgrounds and their needs beyond the immediate transaction. The business officer can only deal with the obvious (a contribution of securities, for instance), and the donor may be more concerned about other matters, such as having the institution thank a spouse immediately.

The business officer works on the organization's financial side. It is difficult for this person, in most situations, to view a problem from the donor's perspective. A situation might arise in which a donor contributes $500,000 worth of stock in a closely held family company. Months later, the business officer is called because the family wants to buy back the securities. Imagine how the donor feels when the business officer wants a premium per share beyond the current market price because the matter is now viewed as one of institutional investment policy. The donor becomes outraged, because there would have been no stock to discuss in the first place unless he or she had contributed it.

Having no knowledge of a situation, the business officer might think that a gift being made is a rather straightforward transaction, when it is actually part of a complicated plan. An experienced development officer, with full knowledge of the matter, would be in a far better position to provide assistance, and could ask the donor:

"Do we understand correctly that you would like this amount applied as the first of three payments against the laboratory your family wants to name in honor of your father?" The donor may well have forgotten for the moment that two more pledge payments will be required.

Knowing that a certain donor usually has his gifts matched by XYZ company, the business officer might want to inquire if the forms for this corporate contribution are being sent. The development officer, who understands the situation, might already know that the donor is using his full limit of corporate support this year to increase gifts to another organization.

It may be difficult for the development officer to convince a business officer that all gifts, donor inquiries, and other communications about contributions should be channeled to the development office immediately. So it becomes an important task of the fund-raising consultants to explain the situation to everyone involved and insist that recommended procedures be followed.

PROSPECTING—ROLE OF RESEARCHERS

Your consultants may be tempted to work with one staff member only, because communication is much simpler that way. But the consultant should be concerned about staff development in the broadest sense. If your staff members remain fixed in their ways, each committed to a narrow activity (prospect research, say, or gift acknowledgement, or proposal writing), they will never see the larger picture and will not be helpful if they are needed in other aspects of the program. For example: If your staff is large, you may have a prospect research director who, working almost in isolation, handles the time-consuming chore of assembling donor profiles for use by solicitors. One day the steering committee asks for "all that stuff you have been putting together" so that "we can get on with our fund-raising calls." But the development director and the consultant have been ignoring this function, and the researcher, who is used to elaborate procedures for gathering information, simply does not know the campaign's timetable and priorities. Consequently, the material is not ready.

The problem could be resolved easily by a consultant and staff leader who bring the research person into planning sessions and, on occasion, to meetings of the steering committee. The person will thus come to understand the campaign's flow and can project realistic research timetables. Of even greater importance, the research person will come to know the key solicitors and vice versa. In practice, the researcher will be more willing to give out information without insisting that no profiles can be released until the last scrap of data has been assembled for a file. In turn, the solicitors will cooperate by adding information to the dossier when they finish the call, thus completing the circle and demonstrating to the researcher that information released to the right solicitor brings back even more information.

SOLICITING—ROLE OF THE PROPOSAL WRITER

You may have a proposal writer who, used to being "faculty-driven," continues as usual to churn out material for foundations and corporations. If the consultant has not taken the time to explain what the campaign's needs will be, the writer will not be ready to cope with special requirements for letters and presentations in the new program. Again, the development director and counsel should provide this important individual with a continuing briefing on campaign planning and progress, as well as a specific timetable for special material. Quite often, the writer will have to deal with the president's office, counsel, and a half-dozen volunteer committee members to make a one-page follow-up letter "just perfect" (meaning at least ten drafts). The writer will accept such assignments with enthusiasm if it is understood from the campaign's outset that such tasks have a great deal riding on them for the organization and when such a letter "wins," counsel can boost staff morale quickly by reaching down into the organization to thank the proposal writer directly. To a professional, praise from a peer—the consultant—can mean more than "thanks" from the volunteer who appreciates what has been done but has no concept of how much hard work went into it.

KEEP YOUR EYE ON THE TARGET

When you have an outside expert in your midst, and the consultant seems to know all of the answers, there will be a temptation to ask for assistance in other areas. "We've got this little problem in the admissions office. Surely you have had experience with that sort of thing." Or "Couldn't you look over our agency's governance process and give us a start by revising the by-laws?" No doubt, an experienced consultant could provide guidance in most of those areas of concern. But remember why the consultant was retained. You want assistance for your major fund-raising effort. Any digression will set the campaign back. Use other experts on other institutional problems; save the fund-raising consultant for fund raising.

Chapter 13

THE FINAL PHASES OF THE CAMPAIGN

> *You've sent us on our way, Mr. Consultant, and we*
> *can carry on alone at this point without further*
> *guidance.*
>
> —A development officer

Now you have your nucleus fund, the campaign has a timetable, the staff is organized, leadership is in place, and solicitors are trained—your campaign is up and running. Campaigns tend to take on lives of their own, progressing in predictable patterns of ups and downs. Counsel's task is to guide the process, smoothing out the peaks and valleys. Volunteers want to know when they can expect certain things to happen. The consultant focuses on completing the campaign activities *in proper sequence* within the general time-frame agreed to by all participants. It boils down to this: If a three-month period has been allotted for solicitation of the nucleus fund but the job is only half finished at the deadline, the committee must complete that phase before going on to the next, no matter what the schedule says. Lack of success in the initial round will lead to lowered sights in the subsequent rounds. Adherence to timetables is important, but not as essential as actual results at each stage of a campaign.

BEYOND THE NUCLEUS FUND

With the nucleus fund drive complete, solicitors now turn their attention to a wider circle of potential donors, designated by several categories according to the size of the gift. The relative importance

115

of each category will be different for large and small campaigns. Table 13-1 illustrates designations for several categories in three campaigns of different size. The designations, percentages, and categories of dollar support shown in the table are arbitrary at best, but they provide guidance from past experience. You will have several good reasons to make adjustments to fit the particular circumstances of your campaign:

- A certain number—18, for example—might have particular symbolic significance for a religious organization; establishing a level at $18,000 instead of at $15,000 might be helpful.

- A precampaign study indicates that the giving constituency varies significantly from the norm: There are several $1 million prospects and then very few others until the $25,000 level is reached; categories and designations should be switched to reflect a realistic appraisal of the situation.

- The board was not put together with fund raising in mind (at a public library, say, where no one could have seen the eventual need for private-sector support); a special campaign council is enlisted, and this group becomes part of the nucleus fund category.

The consultant's task becomes more complex at this stage of the campaign. At the outset the committee will agree to proceed in sequence—nucleus fund and then larger-gift categories first. Moving out in concentric circles from "leadership" through "special" and "general" seems appropriate, but inexperienced volunteers will soon become impatient with the plan. "I just know that we have a thousand friends who want to give $1,000 each right now. Why keep them waiting?" is the comment heard most often. The consultant, resisting this tempting offer, knows that there are not a thousand such donors out there. Even if there were, they should not be seen until larger gifts have been solicited. Counsel must insist that the game plan be followed as pressures build from all sides to change the approach and the staff and experienced committee members, working in support of counsel, must lobby their peers and friends to make certain that the campaign does not roll off its tracks.

TABLE 13-1: Campaign goals of three sample capital campaigns

	TOTAL Campaign Goal		
Designation	**$3,000,000**	**$10,000,000**	**$100,000,000**
Nucleus Fund	(40-60% of total goal)	(30-50% of total goal)	(15-30% of total goal)
	Board (past and present) and a few close friends	same	Add boards of component colleges at a university or special committee members for a large organization
Leadership	$50,000+	$100,000+	$1,000,000+
Major	$15,000+	$ 25,000+	$ 100,000+
Special	$ 3,000+	$ 5,000+	$ 25,000+
Sponsors	—	—	$ 10,000+
General	under $3,000	under $5,000	under $10,000

   During the leadership gifts phase, more often than not, members of the campaign steering committee will begin to complain: "Why do we continue to go over the same darn names at each meeting? Don't we have any other prospects? What's wrong with the research effort in our development operation? Why didn't that consultant pick up more prospect names during the interviews?" Experienced volunteers realize, of course, that the "card value" of those hundred names on the basic list of major gift prospects could well amount to more than 80 percent of the campaign goal. In other words, under preliminary ratings (derived through the interviews, prospect research, and the list reviews by volunteers), the names on that list must be covered if success is to be achieved.

LARGE GIFTS FIRST

Counsel must reassure the committee that the donor list is valid, that others cannot be solicited until gifts are obtained from the first group, and that the staff has done its homework. If the committee moves, for example, from the list of $100,000 candidates and begins to solicit $10,000 prospects, experience from campaigns in which smaller gifts are sought first reveals that several things will occur:

- Prospective donors of $100,000+ will see that most pledges are being made in the $10,000 range; word will circulate within the constituency that "this is obviously a $10,000 campaign."

- Volunteer solicitors will lose heart and become reluctant to ask anyone for much more than $10,000.

- The committee will find it difficult to return to activity at the $100,000 plateau, mostly out of fear that no one will respond now at that level.

- The consultant faces an uphill battle to straighten the course and move the committee back to its proper focus: larger gifts first.

It is risky indeed to reject counsel's advice in this area. Sticking with that "tired list" of the best prospects is crucial. Your campaign should not go beyond this point until every effort has been made to complete all of these vital solicitations.

MONITORING PROGRESS

One way to track how well a campaign is going is to develop a graph (see figure 13-1), based on experience at similar institutions, showing how much an organization hopes to raise in each three-month segment of a two- or three-year program. When the graph is reviewed at each meeting of the campaign committee—with actual progress plotted against projections—everyone involved will be able to see just where things stand.

Another way to monitor progress makes use of two "ticking clocks" that indicate how well an institution is progressing, in time,

FIG. 13.1: **Sample capital campaign progress graph for campaign with $1.75 million goal.**

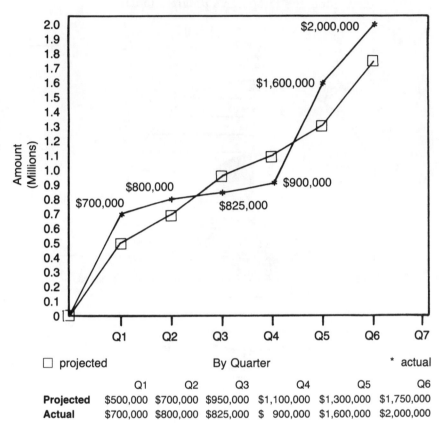

	Q1	Q2	Q3	Q4	Q5	Q6
Projected	$500,000	$700,000	$950,000	$1,100,000	$1,300,000	$1,750,000
Actual	$700,000	$800,000	$825,000	$ 900,000	$1,600,000	$2,000,000

toward its objective (see figure 13-2). The clock would be even more effective if it could be adjusted to allow for the inevitable bulges of large gifts during periods of peak activity and at year's end (both December and June).

When reviewing the campaign's progress in committee meetings, a consultant should never try to figure out who was responsible for raising X dollars in a campaign. There are just two rules to follow: 1) The staff and consultant should never claim credit for gifts received; and 2) the volunteer solicitors are applauded for everything positive that happens.

FIG. 13-2: A "ticking clock" chart of campaign progress. The outer loop illustrates the campaign's projection, while the inner clock plots the campaign's progress to date.

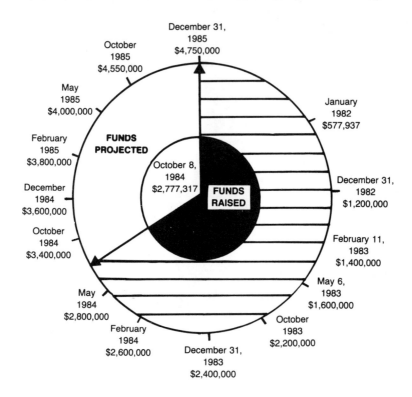

Analyzing Results

Specific yardsticks for assessing progress can be applied by counsel in almost any situation. Three important questions to ask:

- How much better are donors doing in comparison to their pledges in the last drive? If all have doubled what they previously gave, is the organization on the right track?

- How well are individual gifts matching up to what counsel predicted as a result of the study?

• How well are solicitors doing with their assignments when measured by dollar return against what had been projected by counsel and/or a local rating committee?

In one drive for a major university, we suggested that corporations would come through handsomely if the board led the way in an unprecedented fashion. The study responses from trustees indicated that they might well be able to contribute, collectively, three times more than they had given in the last campaign. Corporate leaders were asked to consider doubling their gifts on the condition that trustees would actually pledge three times over what they had done a decade before. It worked. We had agreed, before the procedure began, that there would be no "public" announcement about a campaign or even further consultation with the board about where to set the goal, until we knew if the plan for assembling the initial nucleus fund was valid.

Finally, it is often useful to review regularly counsel's pre-campaign study report. The comprehensive campaign plan should also be gone over regularly and adjusted if need be. The benchmarks in those documents should guide your monitoring of campaign progress. Be careful, however, that such reviews do not turn into scapegoating sessions about counsel's inability to predict what should have happened. Circumstances change, and you want guidance from a consultant who can admit error and help the organization find a proper course.

Why Patience Is Necessary

During a campaign's life, there are times when nothing seems to be happening. When progress is reviewed, it usually turns out that solicitations are not being made or it is taking a long time to develop positive responses from donors. Don't rush things—particularly when a six- or seven-figure commitment is at stake. An old saw has it that every drive is a failure until one day you have a success on your hands. Similarly, every campaign deserves (and usually has) at least one surprise (a major bequest, for instance). An important function of the consultant is to counsel patience.

The chairman of a major preparatory school (not our client) once said that he figured the nine $1 million commitments in his campaign took an average of nine visits each—over a nine-month period—before the pledges were actually made. "I'm convinced that the prospects don't wear out, it's the solicitors who tire. If you persist, and have yet to receive a 'no,' you have a good chance of succeeding if you don't give up."

STEERING COMMITTEE MEETINGS

During a typical campaign, the steering committee may have as many as 35 meetings. If they are not organized and run properly, attendance will slowly dwindle, and you will find yourself at an empty table when the last meeting is held. One hallmark of a successful drive is full attendance at every session.

You should expect a consultant to conduct that first meeting with efficiency and purpose, setting the standard for the campaign to come. A clear, well-planned agenda is absolutely necessary; a sample agenda appears in figure 13-3.

Counsel can guide the planning and execution of these meetings to assure involvement on the part of all who participate—the key ingredient in the effort of maintaining a cohesive committee throughout the campaign. Several "rules" should be enforced by counsel, working in concert with you and your staff:

- Meetings must begin on time and be completed when promised.

- If the agenda cannot be covered in 75 minutes, something should be eliminated.

- The main business of the committee—taking and completing assignments—should be dealt with first at each session.

- Everyone must have an opportunity to participate, from reporting on assignments to commenting on proposed policies.

- All who are involved must leave each meeting with a feeling that "something has been accomplished, and I am eager to get on with my own calls."

- Agendas, with back-up papers, should be circulated a week in advance of a meeting.

FIG. 13-3: A typical steering committee meeting agenda

☑ **1. Progress report on assignments.** Each volunteer reports openly about progress with each assignment card—from how much has been pledged down to needing help for a second visit.

☑ **2. New assignments.** Make certain, first, that the committee isn't moving faster than it should be (have the prospects for the very top gifts been covered?) and that no one is overloaded.

☑ **3. Solicitor training.** Counsel must keep this segment limited to 20 minutes of fast-paced guidance in solicitation techniques through use of playlets involving, in due course, everyone serving on the committee.

☑ **4. Completion of the case statement.** No committee can edit a document; but general comments on the latest draft are needed, and members should be encouraged to return their marked up drafts with specific suggestions on details to the organization's staff.

☑ **5. Policy matters.** A number of suggestions, from additional membership to "what counts?" will be introduced. It is important to circulate background material on any item prior to the meeting—from a list of prospective candidates to a draft statement prepared by counsel.

☑ **6. Review of timetable and budget.** Reminding each other of deadlines never hurts. If the budget report is not reviewed regularly, an aspect of accountability will be lost, and it will be difficult to assure the full board that the committee is doing what it said it would do at the cost originally specified.

☑ **7. Counsel's critical appraisal.** No better use can be made of consultants than having them review, at the end of each meeting, how the campaign is really going—in terms of solicitation problems, deadlines, opportunities, and progress against previously agreed-to benchmarks (e.g., "You are only achieving 75 percent of what we had hoped each card assignment would produce").

☑ **8. Meeting schedule.** Each meeting should end with agreement on when the next one will be held; if you try to do it by telephone later, a long delay will ensue before you are back at the table again. For some organizations, it makes sense to schedule two or three meetings at once.

- Action minutes (who is to do what) should be mailed the day following a meeting, not just barely in advance of the next session.

- It is useful to have the organization's chief executive (president, executive director, headmaster) present at each meeting so that volunteers can say to themselves, "If it's important enough for Joe to be here, it must be important, as he sees it, for the rest of us to be here." And those in attendance can be given a flavor of what is actually happening at the institution.

Two other ingredients can be added to meetings from time to time. So that no one will forget why and in whose behalf the campaign is being conducted, the organization might do well to have a talented caseworker describe a typical situation in which a major problem was solved for a client family by using the organization's funds in a significant way. Or the campaign chairman from a similar organization can be invited to share experiences with the committee—a "what works and doesn't work" seminar. A busy leader of the business community who never accepts outside speaking engagements will almost always agree to talk with others about success in a fund-raising program!

A number of problems in meetings can be avoided if counsel can convince staff to observe some basic rules:

- No one should be expected to bring the papers sent out in advance of a meeting; have duplicate sets ready for everyone, and do not act as if a busy committee member has been irresponsible.

- In addition to sending out reminders about each meeting, members should be called (usually by staff) to assure attendance and to encourage them to complete assignments so that they can give reports that will be encouraging to others.

- The meeting room should be set up properly—always at a table so that materials can be coped with efficiently. Writing pads, pencils, and water should be in place.

- If new papers (revised drafts of things already circulated) are to be used, they should be passed out when needed, not placed in a packet at each person's place. (People will shuffle through the documents when they should be listening to others.)

At the initial meetings of the committee, awkward pauses will develop when it comes time to talk about specific target figures for individual solicitations. And it will be even more awkward, at first, when members wonder whether they should report: "Joe will make a nice gift" or "Joe will pledge at least $50,000." Counsel should lead a discussion, preferably at the first committee meeting, about the importance of being candid and sharing information on a confidential basis within the committee. Most committees will respond well and agree to be open about specific details. Eventually, the committee must know what is really happening. "It's all going well" is inadequate. "We have pledges of $50,000 from Joe, $100,000 from Sam, and a turn-down from Pete for a total of $150,000" is the right way to review progress.

THE EVOLVING ROLE OF THE CONSULTANT

Even the most experienced business leaders wonder if the campaigns they are chairing are really going well, or even if yesterday's meeting really accomplished its purpose. It helps when the consultant calls a day later to review what went well and what did not. Staff can use counsel to focus the drive's leadership on what really must be done this week to activate key committee members who are falling behind in their assignments.

An over-worked development officer might have left the meeting with ten things to do at once (more prospect research, minutes, and telephone calls to people who were not present). Counsel can be of assistance here in sorting out priorities immediately: "Let's get the things out first, so that new assignments are started and we don't find ourselves coming to the next meeting with nothing new to report."

If policy squabbles develop, such as "we don't need a gift-counting statement, decisions can be made as we go along," counsel can suggest patience and the gathering of facts. When committee members know that material developed by similar institutions will be assembled to show that most of the organization's competitors do have formal policies in the area, the dispute will be at an end—at least temporarily.

Part IV
Some Final
Considerations: A
Consultant's View

How much does fund raising cost? How does the consultant look at things? These final, but important, considerations are the focus of Part IV. The issue of cost is discussed from the viewpoint of both the client and the consultant, with some broad guidelines for estimating your own cost. Because harmony and productivity in a client-consultant relationship require an understanding of each other, the final chapter of this book (intended primarily for executives of gift-supported institutions) shares the consultant's perspective on fund raising.

Chapter 14

THE COST OF FUND RAISING

Let's save money by simply finding the least expensive consultant who can do the job quickly.
—A board chairman

CAMPAIGN REQUIREMENTS

How much does it cost to raise funds? As you might imagine, expenses will vary depending on several conditions: whether the campaign is local or national in scope, how large an amount of money is being raised, and whether resident direction is required. While there is no rule of thumb, experience indicates certain guidelines for estimating costs:

- Established annual giving programs cost 10-15 percent of what is raised.

- New annual support efforts might cost 30 percent or more in their formative years.

- Capital campaign expenses (both internal and for counsel) run to about 8-12 percent of proceeds in a drive for $750,000-$1.5 million. If the goal is $3 million or more and the campaign is local, costs can be as low as 3-6 percent.

And how much does it cost to retain fund-raising counsel for a capital campaign? Again, experience offers some reasonable expectations:

129

- If resident direction is required for a capital campaign, counsel's fee (during the campaign) might run between 30 percent and 60 percent of the total amount spent on fund raising (not the total to be raised).

- If ongoing consulting, not resident direction, is required, total charges by the consultant should be in the range of 20-30 percent of the fund-raising budget (with 70-80 percent of the allocation for fund-raising costs applied to staff salaries, publications, special events, travel, and office expenses).

Figure 14-1 breaks out typical expenses for a $5 million dollar campaign without resident direction.

FIG. 14-1: Typical expenses for a $5 million dollar capital campaign without resident direction

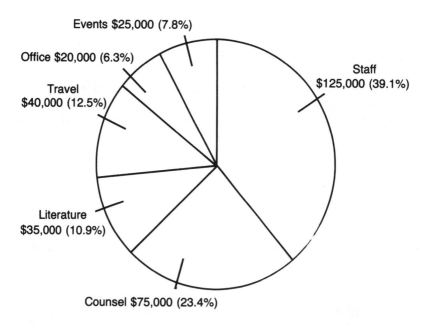

Events $25,000 (7.8%)

Office $20,000 (6.3%)

Travel $40,000 (12.5%)

Staff $125,000 (39.1%)

Literature $35,000 (10.9%)

Counsel $75,000 (23.4%)

A word of caution: Every program has its unique qualities; some causes are more popular than others; staff competence varies; and leadership may or may not require extensive support from the outsider. Budgets and specific costs must be tailored to each situation. General guidelines are starting points only, never a substitute for hard-headed analysis of your own campaign's chances for success and real costs.

Another word of caution: It is false economy to settle for anything less than the best consultant for your campaign. The ideal consultant for your campaign might project charges (covering the study and counseling to follow) of, say, 1.6 percent of the $5 million you hope to raise. Another advisor may well charge fees that amount to 1.4 percent of the campaign's preliminary goal. The appropriate consultant, however, might help the organization raise considerably more than had been anticipated, thus lowering the projected 1.6 percent to only 1.3 percent of the actual proceeds. For an extra expenditure of about $10,000, the institution may be able to raise $6 million rather than $4 million.

HOW CONSULTANTS CHARGE

The Preferred Methods—Time or Project Basis

Reputable consultants are compensated on either a time or project basis. A study fee is normally based on the time devoted to interviewing, case development, and conduct of the internal audit. Campaign consulting charges are usually established on a monthly basis, declining during the period of a drive to reflect a decreasing involvement on counsel's part. As the discussion of the agreement in chapter 7 illustrates, this fee-for-services approach has obvious advantages—everyone knows what is to happen, there will be no "surprise" charges, and specific tasks are purchased with specific amounts of money.

Commission

Years ago, some organizations attempted to develop a commission system which, in the final analysis, created more problems than it solved.

- Commissions were paid on the amount pledged, not paid, because it would be years before all of the funds had actually been given to an organization. Not surprisingly, under that arrangement little concern was given to the quality of the commitments.

- Consultants conducting studies would tend to recommend moving into campaigns because that was the only way they could be paid, even if the evidence gathered dictated a different approach.

- The commission system created conflicts of interest. Often, a thoughtful consultant feels that it would be wrong for the institution to press a prospect for an immediate gift of, say, $10,000 when it was clear that the person might make a bequest later for $500,000. Because no fee is attached to the $500,000 "hope," the consultant is tempted to pursue the $10,000—perhaps losing $490,000 for the organization.

For these reasons, the commission method became so abused that it was discarded and is not used very often these days.

Earning a commission: a consultant's experience. The campaign steering committee for a Washington-based agency was debating how to credit a bequest it had just received. This gift had been made with the stipulation that the income be used only for a purpose in line with the campaign goals. Counsel suggested that the donation be added to the nucleus fund of early gifts from board members and other close friends. Everyone present, except for the agency's president, quickly agreed with the recommendation because bequests are usually counted when they are received during the period of a capital campaign, the restriction attached to the bequest was related to campaign objectives, and having a larger nucleus fund would impress the next round of donors to be asked for pledges.

After the meeting, the organization's president requested a private session with counsel. "You know me," she began, "I always say what is on my mind. And I must tell you that I question counting that bequest when we have to pay you 5 percent of everything raised. By adding this amount to our total, you will receive $12,500 more than you really have coming."

Of course, I was flabbergasted. When I recovered and explained that we had a contract (which she had signed a month earlier) stipulating that my firm was paid a monthly fee for counseling and no commission on proceeds, the president admitted she had forgotten that provision. "It was just fixed in my head that fund-raising consultants were given a percentage of money raised."

If that had been so and if consultants were compensated by commission, it would be difficult to recommend applying special gifts, such as bequests, against campaign goals. In fact, the consultant's hands would be tied on any issue where there was an appearance of conflict of interest.

Per Diem

Many organizations ask consultants to quote a per diem rate, wanting to know if they can purchase consulting on an "as needed" basis. But there are pitfalls in such an arrangement. Consultants must, to a great extent, call the shots. If they waited for an organization to tell them when they were needed, the phone would never ring. This would be particularly so if a daily rate were involved because no one associated with the organization would want to start the meter running. "I guess the problem I have in mind isn't important enough to bother the consultant—especially when the charge will be so great," is what goes through the staff officer's mind.

The per diem concept is also an awkward device for pricing. Can anyone really define what a "day" is? It makes little sense for a consultant to spend eight consecutive hours at a museum or school talking with staff members about the campaign. In reality, the consultant should be spending a few hours on Monday with the development officer, a half-hour on Wednesday chatting with the campaign chairman in California by telephone, and several hours over a long weekend polishing the fourteenth draft of a case statement. Does all of that add up to a "day"? Figure 14-2 at the end of this chapter outlines a recent day I'll not soon forget, and is included to illustrate what a real day in the life of a fund-raising consultant is like.

Monthly Fee

The consultant-client relationship works best if the consultant feels free to take the initiative to set up meetings, visit with the staff development officer, or call a campaign leader who has not come to grips with an important assignment. This feeling will develop best under a monthly fee agreement. The monthly fee covers the gamut of site visits, telephone discussions, the preparation of written documents, and participation in major meetings. Not all of these activities can be anticipated in advance.

Sliding Scale

Some organizations are convinced that a consulting firm will charge smaller institutions on one scale and larger ones on another. "Of course you prefer to work for major universities," they might say, "because you will earn much more than you would in an assignment for our small agency." Unless circumstances are unusual, a firm must give the same time and attention to a smaller organization than it does to the university. In fact, the major institution probably has a large staff of its own and will require less time, in the long run, following a precampaign study. Because fees based on time devoted to an assignment are preferred, you should expect your consultant to charge on one scale, ensuring that all clients are equally important, from a financial viewpoint, to the firm.

Adjusting a fee: a consultant's experience. Although all clients should be charged the same fee for similar services, things do happen that force a consultant to consider an adjustment of rates in a special situation. One evening in northern New England I found myself presenting a report to a small emergency medical service agency on the precampaign study just concluded. Our findings and recommendations had been accepted with enthusiasm, and the discussion had turned to services and fees for continuing counsel during the campaign. Suddenly, from above, a loudspeaker snapped on and I became riveted to my seat as a two-way telephone conversation interrupted us.

"Hurry. Something is terribly wrong; my husband is in great pain."

"Where do you live?"

"Take the first right turn when you reach the mountain in Hillside and go to the very top . . . but hurry, he's turning blue." With that the loudspeaker went dead and the next sound was that of the siren on the ambulance as the vehicle departed from the adjoining garage.

At that moment, life and death were infinitely more important than asking for our regular retainer, and I named a figure that would barely cover expenses. At the end of the meeting, I learned that the ambulance arrived too late. The emergency patient was in full cardiac arrest. This was all in a day's work for the agency. Although I lowered my fee, there was never any reason to wonder if these astute Yankees staged the entire scene, with perfect timing, to soften up the big-city consultant.

Figure 14-2: A day in the life of a fund-raising consultant

5:00 a.m. . . .	awake in Manhattan
6:00 a.m. . . .	picked up by a driver and taken to LaGuardia
7:00 a.m. . . .	commercial flight to Washington
8:00 a.m. . . .	complete arrangements with a cab driver for a full morning's travel through the city
8:30 a.m. . . .	meeting with a prospective client to review material which would be used in a study
9:30 a.m. . . .	study interview with a business leader (who brings three others, unexpectedly, to the session!)
10:10 a.m. . .	a second interview for the same client—across town
10:50 a.m. . .	back to the prospective client for discussion of when a study might begin
11:30 a.m. . .	third study interview
12:45 p.m. . .	back to National Airport; meet charter pilot for flight to Easton, Maryland
1:30 p.m. . . .	met by Trustee of another organization and driven to Oxford, Maryland
2:00 p.m. . . .	study interview started for second client
2:45 p.m. . . .	trustee decides that this is fine time for a second interview with him (for yet another client) so that we won't have to schedule one more meeting
3:00 p.m. . . .	driven back to Easton Airport
3:30 p.m. . . .	charter pilot takes consultant to Suffolk County Airport on Long Island
5:00 p.m. . . .	car rented for half-hour drive to Southampton
6:00 p.m. . . .	meeting with eight museum trustees (prospective client)
7:00 p.m. . . .	drive back to airport
7:30 p.m. . . .	charter pilot heads for Newport, Rhode Island
8:15 p.m. . . .	fog shrouds the airport and we are diverted to Providence
8:45 p.m. . . .	we land in Providence
9:15 p.m. . . .	wife finds husband at a remote corner of the airport
10:00 p.m. . . .	postponed dinner with friends in Newport finally happens
12:00 p.m. . . .	to bed in Little Compton, R.I.

Figure 14-2: A day in the life of a fund-raising consultant (continued)

The scorecard for the day:

- five study interviews completed (but somehow seven people were seen) for three separate clients
- three meetings with two prospective clients
- one commercial flight
- three charter flight segments
- four drivers (including the Washington cabbie and counsel's wife)
- one rental car
- food and drink consumed: three bags of pretzels, eight cups of coffee, two diet sodas and then, finally, dinner!

Chapter 15

FROM THE OTHER SIDE OF THE DESK

> *Something is wrong here. The board members inter-*
> *viewing me don't really have a commitment to their*
> *own cause. They want a campaign just because the*
> *hospital across town is having one.*
> —Consultant realizing that she will have to
> withdraw from consideration

This final chapter looks at fund raising from the consultant's side. Inevitably, some aspects of your relationship with a consultant are adversarial—you have to evaluate prospects, select the one you think is best, negotiate a contract, and, in the worst scenario, find that you have hired the wrong person and must sever ties in the middle of a campaign. But, as this book has emphasized through-out, the client-consultant relationship must be built on mutual respect and trust. This is not a homily; it is a practical fact. That being so, it is helpful for you to understand how consultants think—about you, about themselves, and about financial constraints of their profession.

DO WE REALLY WANT THIS ACCOUNT?

At the same time that a consulting firm is vying for your as-signment, it must take a hard look at itself. Consultants can become adept at "looking good" in interviews and winning accounts. But if it expects to be in business for the long haul, the firm had better be able to back up its promises. Longevity demands a solid reputation.

A firm is looking for trouble when its people say something like this about assigning staff to a prospective client: "Even though Sam has been with our firm for only a year, and has just had real experience with YMCAs, this school's campaign would provide a great training ground for him. Besides, we don't have much for him to do until June." A consultant who makes that statement has more of an eye for his group's bottom line than for the needs of a future client. Trouble is in the offing if:

- the right, experienced staff member is not available for the assignment (in the case of a firm);

- the consultants are too busy to give *this* campaign their full attention;

- the client is viewed as "just a filler" between other, more important assignments; or

- the firm does not perceive the special problems faced by the organization, such as its failure to meet a goal in a recent drive, leadership changes, changes in services provided, or an aging constituency that no longer has much earned income.

Reputable consultants possess their reputations for good reason—they do good work. And they do good work because they are careful to take only assignments that they are equipped to serve. A good fit between client and consultant is as important to the consultant as it is to you. To assure a good fit, a fund-raising consultant should answer these questions:

- Although we know the field (whether it be hospitals, schools, or health agencies), are there potential problems which we are not really equipped to deal with effectively? Would the organization be served better by another consultant?

- Are we trying to assign someone to this account for our own reasons (to gain experience, because a certain staff member is not busy) instead of understanding why someone with special experience and the right temperament is needed?

- Do we have any real interest in either the fund-raising problem faced by the institution or its case? And can we recognize that some firms simply do not perform well in, say, the health area or are not experienced enough with planned giving techniques to understand that this approach must be primary?

- Is our firm effective in situations where no real constituency exists and must be created? Or do we do our best work in more traditional circumstances, with built-in cadres of friends and supporters such as a college's alumni group?

- Will geographical distance present us with obstacles we really cannot overcome in serving this institution?

- Are we kidding ourselves about our ability to deal with the leadership and staff of this organization? Are we deluding ourselves when they tell us they want to combine annual and capital appeals (usually with terrible consequences to the annual program), but we feel they can be persuaded to the contrary later?

- Have we been so polite in our preliminary interview that the organization thinks we will handle the assignment in any way that they suggest or demand?

- Are we willing to stand up, right now, and say that a study is absolutely essential, even though the prospective client insists that it should not be done?

- Have we been enticed to put our best foot forward just because the extent of the proposed assignment is so large that it will create a large income for our firm?

- Are we trying to enter a field in which we have no real experience?

- Finally, and most important for our reputation, will we be promising to deliver something we are not able to do—now or ever?

Much good will can be created for a consultant who says during the first meeting with a selection committee, "Wait a minute, we're on the wrong course. Our firm is not right for this assignment. Let me suggest another way of doing things and three other consultants you should consider."

Turning down an assignment: a consultant's experience. We had once been invited to meet with board members at a hospital in Chicago that had been impressed with our firm because of a successful precampaign interview conducted by one of our vice-presidents with the chairman of the hospital's development committee (on behalf of another institution). As the meeting went along, two things became clear; our firm didn't know enough about hospitals of this size or Chicago's hospital "market" to be helpful quickly, no matter how well we might have carried out the initial study; and geography would be an obstacle because the potential client would need on-site consulting services every day. To go forward with the meeting would have been self-deluding, so we suggested that they consider Chicago-based firms with more experience in hospital fund raising. Soon thereafter, board members met with such a firm and selected it for what has blossomed into a fine relationship.

In another case, a New England school interviewed our firm five years ago for a capital campaign consulting assignment. We sensed that a certain foundation, to which they were linked and which knew our firm well, was prepared to pay all costs for our service through a grant to the school. The school decided that we were not right for them at the moment and that they needed, instead, a low-key consultant who would assist them first in improving annual giving results. We were certain that they were wrong. The foundation agreed with the board, of course, and the grant was used to compensate another firm. Years later, the school approached us again and said that the time for a capital drive had now arrived. We were selected to conduct a study and then to provide counseling. It all worked out very well; the foundation even provided a second grant. The board had been correct from the outset. Earlier, they were not ready for us; the second time around, they were.

WHERE DID WE GO WRONG? REASONS FOR A CONSULTING FAILURE

Most consulting failures stem from precampaign studies. The consultants may have missed the mark for reasons such as:

- They were in too much of a rush to listen carefully to inter-viewees.

- They misinterpreted the answers later.

- They were too eager to hear "the right things."

- They were so emotionally involved in the cause that they would not hear what they were being told.

- They were too friendly with the organization's leadership and didn't want to come in with a negative evaluation.

- They felt they knew the cause, community, and giving climate—no matter what the interviewees seemed to be say-ing of a negative nature.

- They didn't understand the cause at all—or why people did or did not respond to it with dollars regardless of what they said in the interviews.

- They couldn't separate "urgency" from "generalized inter-est."

How do firms and independent consultants guard against such mishaps? By remaining dispassionate and objective—two qualities that make a consultant so valuable to a client. If a consulting firm is competing for a campaign with an adoption agency, a staff member who has recently adopted a child from it is the last person who should be involved in the study. That person could help to write the case, perhaps, but would not be an objective listener in the pre-campaign interviews.

When an organization's leadership is known to the consultant and successful drives have been completed elsewhere for the same individuals, it is important to sit down with these friends and forge some special ground rules for the assignment. One way to say it: "We will tell you what we think, no matter how much it displeases you. Expect the worst and be surprised; don't try to influence us with your biases now or later as we go through the interviews. And we won't let you edit our report to conform with what you would like to have your fellow board members read."

When an assignment will take place in a city familiar to a firm, at least two officers of the firm should conduct the precampaign interviews. One should have no prior experience there.

Finally, if all of the study interviews seem to be producing uniformly positive responses, try recasting the interview format. It is important to encourage a few negative comments by adding a few dissidents to the interviewing sample to make certain that a comprehensive picture of the situation emerges.

By practicing these common-sense safeguards, the consultant, and the client, avoid serious mistakes.

A CONSULTANT ALSO INTERVIEWS THE CLIENT

When interviewing consultants, the selection committee asks hard questions about each one's experience, approach, reliability, and style. In the same way, the consultant will have concerns about you as a prospective client:

1. Is your cause legitimate, e.g., is it legally registered with appropriate government agencies?

2. Do you have (501)(c)(3) status, therefore allowing tax deduction for contributions under IRS regulations?

3. Will the cost of raising funds be excessively high?

4. Is there a voluntary base of interest and support for your endeavor—does anyone out there care?

No one can set a fair ceiling for fund-raising costs, because start-up expenses are always high. Many consultants would be uncomfortable, however, working with an organization that used less than 75-80 percent of contributed support for its goals.

A firm has several methods to check an organization's reputation. The consultant will want to know, for instance, if you use contributions well and have audited statements to back up expenditures; if you conduct programs that appeal to a clearly defined segment of the public; and if your board represents the community it serves. Local United Funds and the Philanthropic Advisory Service of the Council of Better Business Bureaus, among others, keep track of charitable activities and are aware of organizations with poor records of using contributed funds toward the intended purposes.

TESTING THE CASE STATEMENT

During discussions with an organization's selection committee, an astute consultant will look very critically at the case statement, asking for what general objectives the funds are being sought and how, specifically, they will be used. The consultant needs to be satisfied that you know what you are doing. A reputable consultant will be interested in an assignment if the cause is valid, a sense of urgency is present, the goals are compelling, leadership is available, and willing supporters are already identified. Some sign that success is possible is all the consultant is looking for. No firm, after all, wants to build a reputation for failure—or for undertaking studies that rarely lead to fund-raising campaigns.

FINANCIAL CONSIDERATIONS—THE COSTS OF DOING BUSINESS

Consultants want prospective clients to feel that money should not be the crucial point in the selection of counsel. The best consultants cost more than inferior ones, but, argues the consultant, your campaign is too important to leave to the wrong people. Consultants should not seek assignments for the fee alone, and should ask themselves:

- Are we pressing for this assignment only because of the fee? Are they really right for us; are we right for them?

- Will the fee be so substantial that our objectivity will be affected?

- Will the client so dominate our "bottom line" that we won't stand up for what we believe to be the right course of action at every turn?

These are difficult matters for any consultant to deal with objectively. One test: Do total billings to any one organization come to more than 5 percent of a firm's gross billings in one year? If the projection goes beyond that, a firm should be wary.

Consultants often face resistance to their fees. No matter what fee is charged, some members of a selection committee will feel that consultants are overpaid—without regard to how valuable they might be to the organization. But neither that attitude nor the competition for an assignment should tempt a consultant to bid too low to cover costs and provide a fair profit. The actual cost of being in business as a fund-raising consultant is considerable. Some of the expenses are similar to those of any business; others are unique to fund-raising consulting:

- *Taxes* (corporate, personal, state and local business, Social Security, workmen's compensation) can easily take 60 percent right off the top.

- *Registration and bonding fees* can run as high as $200 per year in each state where the firm has clients.

- *New business travel* costs are substantial, and most firms do not charge for initial visits with prospective clients.

- *Legal and accounting fees* add up quickly, often to as much as 3-5 percent of the firm's gross each year.

- *Down time* can be a significant expense, including days lost during a year to inclement weather, participation in professional conferences, and cancellations during a study when interviewees postpone appointments.

- *Office overhead* can be a significant expense when even the smallest firm or individual consultant must lease space on a temporary basis in several cities to meet client needs.

- *Computer and data processing supplies* are a new cost of being in business.

- *Memberships* in such organizations as the AAFRC, National Society of Fund Raising Executives, Council for Advancement and Support of Education, local service clubs, and many more can amount to 2 percent of a firm's gross sales each year.

- *Telephone charges* are always substantial for consultants and are probably double what most professionals pay each year for this service.

- *Subscriptions* mount up quickly and include professional journals, general interest newspapers and magazines, research books, and specialized material on communities in which a consultant is working (maps, atlases, directories, and city magazines).

- *Clothing* is a high personal expense due to wear and tear from constant travel and the obvious need for a neat look.

A consultant's fee is not all gravy—by a long shot.

CONCLUSION

Should consultants resist the temptation to emulate the authors of the best-selling *The One-Minute Manager*? Is it possible to encapsulate advice in easy-to-swallow pills? Can off-the-shelf formulas solve client problems?

By now, having read this book, you know that there are good reasons why fund-raising consultants cannot provide "quick fixes" when prospective or current clients say, "Just tell us how you have done similar projects and base your advice on what has worked elsewhere." If instead, an organization tells a consultant, "Our outfit is unique and we want your advice to be tailor-made for us," the chances for success are high.

It takes time for a successful campaign to be mounted and conducted. An organization's planning, discussed in chapter 3, will require several months. If the selection committee does its job well, two or three months will be required to find the right consultant. Why, then, expect a consultant to reach conclusions and make valid recommendations in a day or a month? Most organizations can make good use of consultants for at least the first 18 months of a two- or three-year capital campaign. When both parties—the consultant and the institution—know that they will be working together that long, it is easier to avoid the temptation of a quick fix and to focus on completing the program in sequence.

Each fund-raising situation has unique facets, and the information provided in this book should be applied as appropriate to yours. "Rules" can not always be followed slavishly, and you and your consultant must be sensitive to the particulars of your donor base personality, demographics, and philanthropic capacity. Two final examples involving library capital campaigns all too clearly illustrate that there is a fine line between when and when not (or perhaps how and how not) to follow the rules.

In the first case, campaigns in adjacent towns that appeared to be similar to the residents of each revealed the wisdom of never using even a part of a publication prepared for another campaign, no matter how similar the two campaigns might seem. Town One's residents included many advertising and publishing executives, artists, and writers. The case brochure developed for their campaign was consequently a bit "flashy" and contemporary graphics were used throughout (lots of white space, several colors, pasted-on elements, etc.). It was successful. The steering committee of Town Two's library campaign thought they might save some time and effort (always an admirable goal) by utilizing Town One's brochure in some way and asked to see it. When they did see it, they were horrified. A second study revealed why. The residents of Town Two were mostly executives in banking, investment banking, and basic industries. The successful appeal to them was one that was simple and direct, and a simple layout with a handsome cover did the job.

The second case involved a steering committee that pressed for a town-wide mailing requesting $1,000 pledges for a place on their new facility's "legacy wall," in defiance of the rule that the largest gifts must be solicited first. The consultant stalled this approach for two months until finally the committee won out and completed the mailing. The prediction from the consultant was that no more than $35,000 would be raised in commitments from 30 donors. To the amazement of all, some 350 gifts of $1,000 or more were made within three weeks, a spectacular return on an 8,000 piece mailing. Why had breaking the rule worked? It was discovered later that the legacy wall concept had become the joke at every dinner party in the community. The question of "Are you on the wall or off the wall?" became the "in" catch phrase, and even those with little interest in the project could not bear to be "off the wall" when the appeal was finally made.

That last story also illustrates the final point to be made, that the consulting arrangement is a collaborative partnership, not a "we-they" confrontation at every turn in the road. It is essential to find the right consultant for you, the one you can work comfortably with, the one who will value your thoughts as much as you welcome and value his professional expertise. Together, you have a long and difficult job to do, and it is only when expectations have been clearly defined on all sides and the plan and approach systematically developed and executed that the consultant, staff, and volunteer leadership can work in harmony toward their shared goal—that of raising funds for the benefit of the cause which your organization serves.

APPENDIXES

The AAFRC

The American Association of Fund-Raising Counsel (AAFRC) is the professional organization of fund-raising consultants, both individuals and firms, in the United States. The association's goal is to promote high standards of professional conduct among its members. Each member subscribes to the AAFRC Fair Practice Code (appearing below with the permission of the AAFRC).

Membership in AAFRC is selective. Before being admitted to the association, a firm's work over the previous three to five years is reviewed. Some 30 firms and individuals are members of the organization.

The AAFRC publishes a directory of its members and an annual report. A fascinating history of the association's first fifty years, entitled *A Beacon for Philanthropy: The American Association of Fund-Raising Counsel through Fifty Years, 1935-1985*, by Wolcott D. Street, is also available.

For further information on the AAFRC, you may call or write to:

The American Association of Fund-Raising Counsel, Inc.
25 West 43rd Street
New York, NY 10036

Telephone: (212) 354-5799

AAFRC FAIR PRACTICE CODE

1. Members of the Association are firms which are exclusively or primarily organized to provide fund-raising counseling services, feasibility studies, campaign management and related public relations, to nonprofit institutions and agencies seeking philanthropic support. They will not knowingly be used by an organization to induce philanthropically inclined persons to give their money to unworthy causes.

2. While the Association does not prescribe any particular method of calculating fees for its members, the Organization should base its fees on services provided and avoid contracts providing for contingency, commissions or a percentage of funds raised for the client.

The Organization should base its fees on high standards of service, and should not profit, directly or indirectly, from the materials or services billed to the client by a third party. Member firms will not offer or provide the services of professional solicitors.

3. The executive head of a member organization must demonstrate at least a six-year record of continuous experience as a professional in the fund-raising field. This helps to protect the public from those who alter the profession without sufficient competence, experience, or devotion to the ideals of public service.

4. The Association looks with disfavor upon firms which use methods harmful to the public, such as making exaggerated claims of past achievements, guaranteeing results, and promising to raise unobtainable sums.

5. No payment, in cash or kind, shall be made by a member to an officer, director, trustee, or advisory of a philanthropic agency or institution as compensation for using his influence for the engaging of a member for fund-raising counsel.

6. In fairness to all clients, member firms should charge equitable fees for all services with the exception that initial meetings with prospective clients are not usually construed as services.

The NSFRE

The National Society of Fund Raising Executives (NSFRE) is a professional organization of more than 6,000 fund-raising executives with its national office in Washington, D.C. and over fifty chapters located in most states and major metropolitan areas. The purpose of the NSFRE is to foster the development and growth of professional fund-raising executives through activities such as chapter and national meetings and educational seminars, and conferences, the provision or career information and a professional certification program, the availability of national staff for consultation and information, and publication of the biannual *NSFRE Journal*, the quarterly *Sightlines*, and the ten-times-a-year *NSFRE News*. The NSFRE also manages and staffs the National Fund Raising Library and resource center, a national repository of information and resource material across the spectrum of the fund-raising field.

Membership in the NSFRE is open to individuals who serve as fund-raising executives for institutions or as members of counseling firms who are engaged in fund-raising management, whose activities are in accord with the Code of Ethics and Professional Practices of the Society (appearing below with the permission of the NSFRE) and its bylaws, and who are recommended by two voting members in good standing of the Society.

For more information on the NSFRE or its chapters, you may call or write to:

The National Society of Fund Raising Executives
1101 King Street, Suite 3000
Alexandria, VA 22314
Telephone: (703) 684-0410

CODE OF ETHICS AND PROFESSIONAL PRACTICES

Preamble

Professional fund raising executives are motivated by positive forces, by an inner drive to improve the society in which they live through the causes they serve. They seek to inspire others through their own sense of dedication and high purpose. They are committed to the improvement of their own professional knowledge and skills in order that their performance will better serve others.

They recognize their trusteeship — to assure their employers that needed resources are vigorously sought, and donors that their purposes in giving are honestly fulfilled. Such professional write their own code of ethics every day.

Professional Fund Raising Executives Accept and Abide By The Following Code of Ethics and Professional Practices:

1. Members shall be responsible for conducting activities in accord with accepted professional standards of accuracy, truth, integrity and good faith.

2. Members shall encourage institutions they serve: to conduct their affairs in accordance with accepted principles of sound business management, fiduciary responsibility, and accounting procedures; to use donations only for the donors' intended purposes; and to comply with all applicable local, state, provincial and federal laws.

3. Members shall manage all accounts entrusted to them solely for the benefit of the organizations or institutions being served.

4. Members shall recommend to the institutions they serve only those fund raising goals which they belive can be achieved based on their professional experience, and an investigation and rational analysis of facts.

5. Members shall work for a salary, retained or fee, not a commission. If employed by a fund raising organization that organization shall operate in its client/consultant relationship on the basis of a predetermined fee and not a percentage of the funds raised.

6. Members shall make full disclosure to employers, clients or, if requested, potential donors all relationships which might pose, or appear to pose, possible conflicts of interest. As fund raising executives they will neither seek nor accept "finder's fees."

7. Members shall hold confidential and leave intact all lists, records and documents acquired in the service of current or former employers and clients.

8. A member's public demeanor shall be such as to bring credit to the fund raising profession.

GLOSSARY

AAFRC. American Association of Fund-Raising Counsel, Inc., the New York-based organization to which 31 of the major consulting firms in the field belong.

ANNUAL CAMPAIGN. See ANNUAL FUND DRIVE.

ANNUAL FUND DRIVE. An effort to solicit contributions on a yearly cycle to cover a gift-supported institution's operating expenses (the difference between income and expenses). Also know as a BUDGET or MAINTENANCE drive, and in churches as an EVERY-MEMBER CANVAS.

ANNUAL GIVING. Contributions made in response to the annual fund drive.

BUDGET DRIVE. See ANNUAL FUND DRIVE.

BOARD. As in "the board," refers to the board of trustees of a gift-supported institution or organization.

CAMPAIGN. Any type of fund-raising effort that involves solicitation of direct contributions to achieve a monetary goal, as opposed to a special event which raises funds by such means as raffles, sale of a table at a benefit dinner, and so on.

CAMPAIGN PLAN. A comprehensive schedule, budget, and strategy statement prepared at the outset of a major fund-raising drive.

CAPITAL CAMPAIGN. Usually a three- to five-year program in which pledges, payable over that time period, are sought for such objectives as construction projects, renovations, and endowment.

CASE. See CASE STATEMENT.

CASE STATEMENT. The long-range plan for a gift-supported organization, presented in a fund-raising context, that sets forth, in generally no more than 12-15 pages, the organization's history, where it stands now, its plans for the future, the difference that contributed funds will make in realizing those plans, and how the funds will be obtained.

CONSULTANT. In the fund-raising context, an individual (or a firm) who applies proven fund-raising research methodology and management principles to assist and guide a gift-supported organization in achieving its fund-raising objectives without actually soliciting contributions. A consultant provides either RESIDENT DIRECTION or continuing counseling with frequent site visits.

COUNSEL. See CONSULTANT.

DEFFERED GIVING. See PLANNED GIVING.

DEVELOPMENT. The art of cultivating prospective donors and obtaining their support; the term is often used to describe the fund-raising staff function within a gift-supported institution.

DONOR. The source of a gift or pledge; may be an individual, corporation, or foundation.

ENDOWMENT CAMPAIGN. A capital campaign with a decided focus on endowment—funds that will be invested to produce yearly income for operating expenses.

EVERY-MEMBER CANVASS. See ANNUAL FUND DRIVE.

EXECUTIVE SEARCH. Use of a consultant who specializes in finding executive-level staff, most often the head development officer but also others such as a finance office, database administrator, or proposal writer.

FEASIBILITY STUDY. See PRECAMPAIGN STUDY.

FUNGIBLE. Legal term designating movable goods, any part of which can replace another part, as in money used to discharge a debt. In fund-raising, used to describe a situation, for example, in which donors to a school prefer to contribute toward scholarship aid, thus creating a campaign shortfall in funds for faculty compensation. The institution needs less from its operating budget for scholarships and money is freed within this budget for increased faculty compensation.

GIFT. An outright contribution of money, securities or other property. Also, a payment toward a multi-year pledge. See also PLEDGE.

GIFT-SUPPORTED INSTITUTION. Contemporary term for a nonprofit, tax-exempt organization. Donors to it are able to deduct contributions from their income tax returns as charitable contributions. Often called (501)(c)(3) organizations, referring to their designation in the tax code.

INTERNAL AUDIT. Consultant's review of an institution's fund-raising staff and procedures to assess the organization's readiness for a major campaign. See also PRECAMPAIGN STUDY.

MAINTENANCE DRIVE. See ANNUAL FUND DRIVE.

NSFRE. National Society of Fund Raising Executives, a Washington-based organization to which more than 6,000 development officers belong.

NUCLEUS FUND. A "kitty" established at the outset of a campaign, usually limited to board members who make early gifts at levels that serve as examples for others.

PLANNED GIVING. Contributions generally not transferred immediately to a gift-supported institution, such as gifts made by bequest, life insurance beneficiary clauses, and more complex gifts that, in exchange for the contribution, return to the donors or their heirs an interest in or income from the gift for a specified time.

PLEDGE. A commitment to make a contribution that will usually be paid over a period of three or more years.

PRECAMPAIGN STUDY. The first phase of a CAMPAIGN, consisting of two parts: feasibility tests to determine if the preliminary goals can be achieved, and the internal audit to evaluate the organization's capabilities for a successful campaign.

PROSPECT RESEARCH. A systematic approach assessing prospective donors' interests and abilities to contribute.

RECONNAISANCE STUDY. A short study by a consultant, encompassing confidential interviews with volunteer leaders (see also VOLUNTEER) and prospective donors to assess a campaign's progress at mid-point and to determine if adjustments are required.

RESIDENT DIRECTION. Refers to the coordination and overall management of a campaign by an on-site consultant.

SECOND STUDY. See RECONNAISANCE STUDY.

SOLICITOR. One, usually a volunteer, who asks others to support an institution or a case. See VOLUNTEER.

STEERING COMMITTEE. The leadership group, usually including a number of key board members, responsible for both the policy-setting and major solicitations in a fund-raising program.

TELEMARKETING. Also known as telefundraising. The efficient, organized, and cost-effective method for reaching   donors or clients in an effort to increase giving or sales. Ordinarily, paid telephone callers solicit support after a series of letters has been used to explain the case.

VOLUNTEER. One who gives time freely in support of an institution or a cause. They are crucial in any fund-raising program.

SIMPLIFIED CAMPAIGN AGENDA INDEXED BY CHAPTER

The following agenda indicates the broad steps of a campaign and in which chapter(s) they are covered.

Campaign step	Covered in chapter(s)
☐ Determine the need for a campaign.	1, 3
☐ Compose a first draft of the case statement.	2, 3
☐ Select a consultant.	3-8, 14-15
☐ Conduct the precampaign study (feasibility and internal audit), refine case statement, determine special needs and campaign goals.	2, 8, 9, 15
☐ Accept precampaign study reports, determine whether to proceed.	9
☐ Develop final campaign goals/plans/ timetable, organize steering committee, development staff, and volunteers as necessary; research prospects; complete case statement.	10-13
☐ Solicit contributions to the nucleus fund.	10
☐ Make final review of campaign goals/plan/ timetable, staffing.	10-13
☐ Make the public announcement.	10
☐ Carry out the campaign.	10-conclusion

BUILD YOUR FUND-RAISING LIBRARY

FUND RAISING RESEARCH REFERENCES

TAFT BASIC II SYSTEM
The ultimate fund-raising resource covering the charitable giving of America's largest foundations and corporations. Consists of a one-year subscription to the Taft Corporate Information System and the Taft Foundation Information System. *(components available separately)*

TAFT CORPORATE INFORMATION SYSTEM
Detailed coverage of America's major corporate giving programs—both corporate foundations and direct giving programs. Includes annual 850-page hardbound *Taft Corporate Giving Directory*—biographical data on trustees and officers and current, comprehensive analyses of contributions programs. Exhaustively indexed. Supplemented with monthly newsletters, *Corporate Giving Watch/Corporate Giving Profiles. (components available separately)*

TAFT FOUNDATION INFORMATION SYSTEM
Detailed coverage of America's major private foundation giving programs. Includes *Taft Foundation Reporter*—annual 800-page hardbound directory with biographical data on foundation trustees and comprehensive reports and analyses of foundation giving programs. Exhaustively indexed. Supplemented with monthly newsletters, *Foundation Giving Watch/Foundation Giving Profiles. (components available separately)*

CORPORATE GIVING YELLOW PAGES: Philanthropic Contact Persons for 2,000 of America's Leading Public and Privately Owned Corporations
Here are hundreds of corporate direct giving programs and corporate foundations *not covered in any other resource!* Lists sponsoring company, contact person, address, and phone number. Indexed by location and type of industry.

AMERICA'S WEALTHIEST PEOPLE: Their Philanthropic and Nonprofit Affiliations
An invaluable complement to *People in Philanthropy*, this directory focuses in even greater detail on the charitable habits of America's rich. Over 500 in-depth profiles couple biographical data with philanthropic, nonprofit, and corporate affiliations.

PEOPLE IN PHILANTHROPY: A Guide to Nonprofit Leadership and Funding Connections
In demand since its release, this unique, biennial directory contains biographical data on the thousands of individuals who control philanthropy in the corporate and foundation world, as well as profiles of many of America's wealthiest individuals.

CORPORATE PHILANTHROPY IN AMERICA: New Perspectives for the Eighties
This Taft Special Report analyzes corporate giving in this decade, telling you *the* nine reasons corporations give, where the money goes by industry and by area of activity, and what the future holds in terms of trends, increases, or decreases. Bibliography and tables included make this an invaluable resource for updating your fund-raising plans and strategies.

NEWSLETTERS

THE NONPROFIT EXECUTIVE
Action-oriented monthly newsletter for nonprofit managers. The first newsletter dedicated to advancing the careers of executive-level nonprofit managers and development officers. Your way of keeping in touch with all the trends, new development ideas, events, and concepts that affect your performance and success. Features a special careers/jobs section.

CORPORATE GIVING WATCH
With corporate giving now clearly the fastest growing segment of philanthropy, the successful development director seeking corporate funds needs plenty of useful intelligence on the corporate giving scene—on the individual companies, their executives, and their giving. *Corporate Giving Watch* is the *only* newsletter designed expressly to deliver all this crucial information—and in a comprehensive yet concise format.

FOUNDATION GIVING WATCH
It's a fact of life in fund raising that most foundations do not do a very good job of informing the public about their activities. You can be sure that decisions are being made all the time which affect your chances of getting foundation grants. *That's why you need Foundation Giving Watch*—a monthly newsletter devoted to telling you the news about foundations and, most important, what it means to you.

COMPUTER RESOURCES—NEW FROM TAFT

BASIC COMPUTER KNOWLEDGE FOR NONPROFITS:
Everything You Need To Know Made Easy
This new manual distills all the vital knowledge you need *before* you explore computerizing your nonprofit organization. Its easy-to-use format takes you through definitions, discussions, and applications of hardware, software (word processing, database management, spreadsheets, telecommunications), needs assessment, and alternatives to full computerization. All geared exclusively to the nonprofit marketplace. Contains worksheet forms and glossary.

TEAM SYSTEM®DEVELOPMENT PACKAGE
This innovative fund-raising software produces mailing lists, phone lists, thank-you letters, gift receipts, campaign analyses, grant analyses, cash receipt summaries, donor histories, bio sheets, prospect lists, and more.

Use your in-house microcomputer to store complete profile information on key people—donors, board members, grant makers, volunteers—anyone with whom you need to maintain close contact. The TEAM SYSTEM database stores complete data for their name, address, phone, personal interests, demographics, and every gift, grant, proposal, or payment you've received from them.

Requires a hard-disk storage system. Runs on any MS-DOS Version 2 or greater microcomputer (including IBM, Digital, and Wang PCs). Software, User's Guide, training diskettes, and training manual are only $1,350. Or try our no-risk demo package for only $39.95, available for hard-disk and floppy-disk systems. If you're not convinced TEAM SYSTEM will improve your ability to raise funds and manage donors, return the demo within 30 days of purchase for a full refund.

"TEAM SYSTEM" is a registered trademark of Burt Woolf Management, Inc.

PROFESSIONAL BOOKS (new releases *)

*CAREERS IN THE NONPROFIT SECTOR: Doing Well by Doing Good

How do you make it to the top (or get your foot in the door) of this $150 billion industry? This book explodes many a myth about the third sector as it explores job opportunities, competition, and trends from job search to interview to future prospects. Includes interviews with top nonprofit professionals, a listing of top nonprofits, worksheets, and a job checklist.

CONFESSIONS OF A FUND RAISER: Lessons of an Instructive Career

A heartwarming, uplifting, funny, candid and revealing memoir from Maurice G. Gurin, the "elder statesman of the fund-raising profession." Chronicles his remarkable career as fund-raising consultant to some of America's most well-known philanthropists and institutions.

DEAR FRIEND: Mastering the Art of Direct Mail Fund Raising

For the experienced practitioner or those just getting started in raising funds by mail. Written by principals of the renowned Oram Group, Kay Partney Lautman and Henry Goldstein. The outstanding how-to guide.

DO OR DIE: Survival for Nonprofits

For the nonprofit executive who recognizes the advantage of "profit thinking for nonprofit organizations." Insightful exploration of nonprofit management approaches—separates myth from fact.

*HOW TO HIRE THE RIGHT FUND-RAISING CONSULTANT: And Make the Most of Your Campaign

From precampaign planning through a campaign's final phases, this book shares the tips and secrets of planning, interviewing, negotiating, and working with a fund-raising consultant to create that often elusive chemistry needed for a successful campaign. Presents how-to techniques and checklists punctuated with illustrative anecdotes; also includes sample letters, agendas, agreement form, schedules, glossary.

HOW TO RATE YOUR DEVELOPMENT OFFICE: A Fund-Raising Primer for the Chief Executive

Outstanding guide covering every detail needed to clarify and assess the success of your development office. Superb manual for every chief executive—whether you're planning to institute a new development program or looking to make your current fund-raising office more productive.

*MANAGING CONTRIBUTED FUNDS AND ASSETS: The Tax-Exempt Financial Planning Manual

By means of an ingenious system of actual ledger worksheets and explanatory text, the author takes you through the accounting and financial planning steps needed to maximize cash, increase yields, and build endowment. More than just a manual system, the application of the information and techniques presented will also improve reporting practices and procedures within your organization. Purchase includes blank ledger worksheets for your use.

★ ★ ★ ★ ★ TAFT'S FIVE-STAR FUND-RAISING PACKAGE ★ ★ ★ ★ ★

UP YOUR ACCOUNTABILITY: How to Up Your Funding Credibility by Upping Your Accounting Ability

The first nontechnical accounting "textbook" ever written specifically to meet the needs of the nonprofit manager or student. Gives you the basic information you need to understand the financial workings of a nonprofit group and to do realistic financial planning.

THE 13 MOST COMMON FUND-RAISING MISTAKES and How to Avoid Them

This down-to-earth, witty, cartoon-illustrated book shows how adherence to a few basic principles can yield more grants, more gifts, more wills and bequests. Written by Paul H. Schneiter and Donald T. Nelson, it draws on exceptional experience in legendary Mormon fund-raising circles.

BUILDING A BETTER BOARD: A Guide to Effective Leadership

For every board member or nonprofit executive interacting with trustees, this succinct booklet will help you gain maximum board effectiveness through understanding the roles and expectations of each and every board member. Written by Andrew Swanson who brings over 25 years of practical working experience as president or trustee on more than 30 nonprofit boards.

THE PROPOSAL WRITER'S SWIPE FILE: 15 Winning Fund-Raising Proposals

The grants-oriented fund raiser's "best friend" in helping design successful applications. Pattern your proposals on these examples of actual winning proposals.

PROSPECTING: Searching out the Philanthropic Dollar

The most comprehensive functional manual on donor research available today, covering every major aspect of prospect research. Includes valuable Forms Kit enabling you to conveniently record your prospecting research.

The above five valuable learning tools for one special price.

Qty.	Publication	Price	P&H
	FUND RAISING RESEARCH SYSTEMS		
____	□ **Taft Basic II System · 1986** (Includes *Taft Corporate Information System* and *Taft Foundation Information System*) *(Regular price $734) Save $137!*	$597.00	$25.00
____	□ **Taft Corporate Information System · 1986** (Includes *Taft Corporate Giving Directory* and *Corporate Giving Watch / Corporate Giving Profiles) Save $47!*	$367.00	$15.00
____	□ **Taft Foundation Information System · 1986** (Includes *Taft Foundation Reporter* and *Foundation Giving Watch / Foundation Updates) Save $30!*	$367.00	$15.00
	FUND RAISING RESEARCH DIRECTORIES		
____	□ **Taft Corporate Giving Directory** (1986 ed.)	$287.00	$10.00
____	□ **Taft Foundation Reporter** (1986 ed.)	$287.00	$10.00
____	□ **People In Philanthropy** (1984-1985 ed.)	$187.00	$10.00
____	□ **America's Wealthiest People: Their Philanthropic and Nonprofit Affiliations**	$57.50	$5.00
____	□ **Corporate Giving Yellow Pages** (1986 ed.)	$67.50	$5.00
	NEWSLETTERS		
____	□ **Corporate Giving Watch / Corporate Giving Profiles** · one year (12 issues) *(Regular price $127) Save $30*	$97.00	
____	□ **Foundation Giving Watch / Foundation Updates** One year (12 issues) *(Regular price $127) Save $30*	$97.00	
____	□ **Nonprofit Executive** One year (12 issues)	$97.00	
	Charter subscription (still available)	$77.00	
	PROFESSIONAL BOOKS		
____	□ **Basic Computer Knowledge for Nonprofits**	$67.50	$10.00
____	□ **Building a Better Board: A Guide to Effective Leadership**		
	1 - 4 copies—each at	$9.50	$2.25
	5 - 9 copies—each at	$5.50	$5.00
	10 or more copies—each at	$3.50	$10.00

Qty.	Publication	Price	P&H
____	□ **Careers in the Nonprofit Sector: Doing Well By Doing Good**	$19.95	$3.(
____	□ **Confessions of a Fund Raiser**	$24.95	$3.(
____	□ **Corporate Philanthropy in America: New Perspectives for the Eighties**	$27.00	$2.2
____	□ **Dear Friend: Mastering the Art of Direct Mail Fund Raising**	$47.50	$5.0
____	□ **Do or Die: Survival for Nonprofits**	$13.95	$2.2
____	□ **How to Hire the Right Fund-Raising Consultant**	$24.95	$3.0
____	□ **How to Rate Your Development Office**	$21.95	$3.0
____	□ **Managing Contributed Funds and Assets**	$167.00	$10.(
____	□ **The Proposal Writers Swipe File**	$18.95	$2.2
____	□ **Prospecting: Searching out the Philanthropic Dollar**	$23.95	$2.:
____	□ **Taft's Five Star Fund-Raising Package**	$75.95	$10.(
____	□ **The Thirteen Most Common Fund-Raising Mistakes**	$17.95	$2.
____	□ **Up Your Accountability**	$15.95	$2.'

TEAM SYSTEM Software

Qty.		Price	P&H
____	□ TEAM SYSTEM Development Package	$1,350.00	$10.(
____	□ Special Demo Package	$ 39.95	$3.

Please indicate your
- computer brand and model: _____
- installed RAM: _____ K • MS-DOS version # _____
- how many names you wish to store (approx.)_____